DUCT TAPE
& WD-40

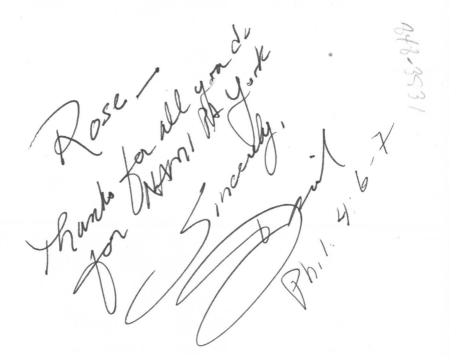

Rose —

Thanks for all you do
for OHSN! At York

Sincerely,

Phil. 4:6-7

DUCT TAPE & WD-40

A parent's guide to the mysteries of a bipolar child.
When the "fix-it" approach doesn't work.

David Anderson Brown

foreword by Newt Gingrich

Published by Advantage, Charleston, South Carolina.
Member of Advantage Media Group.

ADVANTAGE is a registered trademark and the Advantage colophon is a trademark of Advantage Media Group, Inc.

Printed in the United States of America.

ISBN: 978-1-59932-090-8
LCCN: 2008943882

This publication is designed to provide accurate and authoritative information in regard to the subject matter covered. It is sold with the understanding that the publisher is not engaged in rendering legal, accounting, or other professional services. If legal advice or other expert assistance is required, the services of a competent professional person should be sought.

Most Advantage Media Group titles are available at special quantity discounts for bulk purchases for sales promotions, premiums, fundraising, and educational use. Special versions or book excerpts can also be created to fit specific needs.

For more information, please write: Special Markets, Advantage Media Group, P.O. Box 272, Charleston, SC 29402 or call 1.866.775.1696.

Visit us online at **advantagefamily**.com

This book is dedicated to

My daughter Emily M. Egan

Whose very life has affected my life in ways far beyond my expectations. Thank you, Emily, for allowing me to share our story.

Emily's mother, Roberta K. Brown

Whose love of family often sustained us through all the trials and tribulations associated with parenting a child suffering from Bipolar Disorder.

Emily's sister and our daughter, Susan E. Brown

Whose love of life and passionate pursuit of her God given talents continues to inspire me in more ways than she will ever know.

David Brown has written an intimate, personal, and courageous book. As his brother in law, and as Emily and Susan's uncle and Rob's brother, I know personally how difficult and challenging this period of pain, discovery, and hope was for the entire Brown family.

Our Mother had experienced both depression and bipolar disorder and we had all had to come to grips with the fact that someone you love can find themselves overwhelmed by impacts you do not understand, cannot predict, and may not be able to change.

I had a cousin who had ruined his life with drugs in his early twenties and spent the rest of his too short life going in and out of mental hospitals and living in structured housing.

With this background the concern for Emily was real, overwhelming, and deeply human. Everyone involved knew that this was a very difficult period and its outcome was uncertain. Everyone knew that they loved Emily and she loved them but love might not be enough by itself. Everyone was more than a little afraid and very uncertain what to do and how to work toward a positive future.

The power of David's book for any other family faced with these challenges is its very honesty and the pain and confusion it accurately communicates. This will give you, the reader, permission to surface your own pain and to be honest about your own confusion.

Emily has acted courageously in giving her father permission to tell this personal and difficult story. Rob and Susan have been supportive in trying to find a way to help others through this act of witness. I hope that everyone who is in need of help will find this book useful.

I hope every citizen who wants to know more about the challenge of these kinds of problems will find this book enlightening.

I know that for David and Emily this was a journey of pain and discovery, of fear and love, and that it is a journey, which will bind them for the rest of their lives. Now, you have a chance to make it a part of your life's journey also.

—Newt Gingrich

ACKNOWLEDGEMENTS

I was somewhat hesitant to write these acknowledgements out of fear I would miss someone who either helped develop this finished product or encouraged me along the way. After all, the whole process of writing, editing and publishing stretched out over 5 years. That being said, allow me to acknowledge these very special people.

Long before this story begins, my friend and mentor, Charlie "Tremendous" Jones began to encourage me to write a book. He seemed to have faith in my abilities long before I did. More than that, Charlie was the one who introduced me to my Lord and Savior, Jesus Christ. My friend, Charlie, entered God's Greater Kingdom in October of 2008.

The writing of this book began with the encouragement of Brad Bumsted, a political journalist and friend from church. Brad offered to help in the editing process as a way of encouraging me to take on the task.

Dan Flint, a friend from church, is the man responsible for my attendance at a Promise Keeper's Event which changed my prayer life forever. This book is a direct response to answers to prayer which unfolded as a result of my new disciplined prayer life.

You will meet my friend, Bob, as you read. Bob (whose last name I choose to keep anonymous out of respect for his own struggles with recovery) was the one person who got me to see just how damaging my method of fathering was to Emily's chance for recovery. I'm sure others had tried. Bob was the one who broke down the wall I had built around myself keeping me from hearing things I needed to hear. Bob suffers from Bipolar Disorder. He has been there. No one else had that credential.

Dona Constantine from Orange County, California was the only person to tell me about NAMI (National Alliance for Mental Illnesses). I was in desperate need for some kind of support and education. It took the love of a woman I had only met on a couple of occasions, a woman who lives on the other side of the country, to reach out with the information I needed. Once I attended my first NAMI support meeting, I quickly learned that NAMI is a community of loving and caring people, always willing to help when and where they could. That's why it was such a natural thing for Dona to reach out to me in my time of need. There are so many people in NAMI who have reached out to me personally; it does not allow my naming them all. Dona was the one who opened the door to NAMI for me hence making her the exception.

Dr. David Roquemore became pastor of my church a couple of years into Emily's and my journey together. Unfortunately, he was not our pastor when Emily was first hospitalized. Unlike other pastors, I was able to talk with David about the pain I was experiencing, emotionally and spiritually, without feeling misunderstood. We began to build a friendship that is still growing strong today.

Vonny Getz served as my Executive Assistant during the most challenging years of my life as Emily's father. When I told Vonny that Brad had encouraged me to write this book, she immediately volunteered to assist in any way she could. Vonny was very much a part of bringing this book to life.

Tucker Thompson, known by friends as "Friar Tuck", helped bring this book to its conclusion. His famous "red penned" editorial comments helped me narrow the focus, bringing greater clarity and understanding to all that was written.

Roger M. Cadieux, MD has served our extended family over many years. Roger is the only Psychiatrist who took the time to help me understand the mysteries behind the behaviors of my mother-in-law, and of course, my daughter, Emily. Roger, too, was an early encourager as I spoke about writing this book.

I'm appreciative of Keith Ayers, President and CEO of Integro Leadership Institute, friend and mentor, for allowing me to use the Whole Person model in the writing of this book, and for his encouragement and help in finding a publisher.

I am blessed to have had a brother-in-law who, in spite of his notoriety, would take the time to do whatever he could to help his sister and her family as we struggled with so many challenging issues. Not only is Newt Gingrich one of the nation's most brilliant leaders, he is a loving and caring brother and uncle.

Finally, this book would have never seen the light of day without the permission of my daughter, Emily, and the loving support of her mother, Rob Brown.

WHERE IT ALL BEGAN

Ever since May 18, 2000 I have thanked God every day for sparing my daughter Emily's life; by telling her to pick up the phone and call 911.

It is 2004 and I awoke this morning and life is beautiful. A month or so ago, life was not so beautiful. What changed? The world hadn't changed. The world is pretty much the same from day to day with the exception of the weather patterns, and unforgettable significant events such as the day a child is born. Other than that why is it some days are beautiful, and others are so ugly? If the world hasn't changed, what changed? It must be me!

We have to continually look at our self and ask the question, "Where am I on this journey, I call my life?" If we imagine life as a river than the question becomes where am I on my "river of life"?

Years ago, I was leading a YMCA staff retreat at a beautiful outdoor resident camp. I had given the staff an assignment to work on which would take them the better part of an hour. I decided to take advantage of this free time and went for a walk on the camp's grounds.

There was a beautiful outdoor chapel next to a slow moving stream. There was a pulpit built of mountain stone with a large wooden cross in the background and several rows of park benches serving as the sanctuary. The entire chapel was open air, covered only by the boughs of tall pine trees.

I sat in the front row, simply enjoying the ambiance of the setting when something caught my eye. A large tree which hung out over the stream appeared as if it were on fire. I sat there in awe of what I was seeing, questioning, for a split second, if this was some spiritual experience. "Was God really about to speak to me?" It didn't take me long to realize that what I was seeing was the reflection of the sunlight off the water as it rippled under the tree, causing the tree to appear as if it were on fire.

It was the type of setting that offered a period of deep introspection. Having walked over to the stream, I stared down at the deep pool of water under the tree. Although the water seemed to flow smoothly and peacefully, you could tell by the sound that not too far up stream this same water flowed through some turbulent areas creating rapids, or "white water." This same stream, which recently came through turbulence, was currently calm. Yet, it would soon face another series of obstacles creating turbulence once again. And such is life.

Emily was our miracle child. She arrived in this world June 8, 1986, after an eleven-year struggle with infertility. Our struggles were over, so we thought. Life was calm. Five weeks later my eighty-three-year-old father had a stroke, which a few months later, took his life. Life was turbulent, followed by an eventual calm once again. Calm waters leading to free and fast flowing waters. Here and there were a few white water rapids, but nothing we couldn't handle.

Then came 1988, the worst year of our married lives, at least up to that point.

Our daughter, Susan, was to enter this world on March 15th. Life was exciting, yet not turbulent, that is until she arrived six weeks early. Because she was premature, her first week of life was in the neo natal intensive care unit. Susan was released to our care wearing a monitor around her chest as a safe guard for potential Apnea concerns. Caring for an infant who must wear a monitor for potential Apnea twenty-four/seven was turbulent. But that turbulence was minor compared to the white waters that hit us next.

My mother-in-law, Kit, began to act in a somewhat strange manner. She lived twelve miles away and was an important part of our lives, frequently caring for our children. Rob (short for Roberta) was a stay-at-home mother, yet we always welcomed Kit's help. Kit was always reliable, and like most grandmothers, very nurturing and fun to be with.

Gradually, and without warning, her behaviors began to change. She would stop on her way to our home to shop… for hours on end. This was before the days of cell phones, so we would have no idea where she was. This of course led to hours of worry and concern on our part. To Kit, it was no big deal. Shopping was important.

Then she started to leave her own home late at night and spend hours at a local twenty-four-hour restaurant, drinking coffee and smoking cigarettes. The coffee and cigarettes were normal; it was the hour of the day, and the sitting in a restaurant that was unusual.

She was far more irritable then usual, becoming angry at the slightest incident. My father-in-law, Bob, said he felt as if there were only two things wrong according to Kit: everything he did and everything he said.

It wasn't long before she started to call the state police late at night, accusing my father-in-law of threatening to harm her. There were nights we found out later that she would leave home and go visit Candy's friends. Candace, as she prefers to be called today, is my youngest sister-in-law. She was living at home during summer break from college, and was beside herself with her mother's unpredictable and frustrating behaviors.

Then the late night phone calls started. "David, I don't feel well. Will you come and take me to the hospital?" The first such call came around four in the morning. I asked if Bob was at home, and, if so, couldn't he take her? "Bob? The son of a bitch is sitting right here. I wouldn't ask him if he were the last person on earth!" This was not at all like the Kit I knew. Then I asked if Candy was home. "Candy? David, she's sound asleep. You don't want me to wake her, do you?" "You're damn right I do!" I hung up.

A similar call came a couple days later. This time I said, "Kit, I'll be right there." Fifteen hours later we had Kit admitted into a psychiatric hospital unit.

My college degree is in psychology, but I had never observed someone suffering from a form of mental illness first hand. When the doctors told us that Kit was suffering from an extreme manic episode associated with bipolar disorder I sat there in disbelief. Yes, Kit was acting strangely, but bipolar disorder? What was that?

You talk about white water rapids on the river of life. Our whole extended family was in shock.

Then there was 1991. My wife, Rob, is now a fifteen-year breast cancer survivor. For two years, beginning with her diagnosis and mastectomy, our life was turbulent. I had lost my father. Was I now going to lose my best friend? Then, as time passed, things calmed down and we were able to enjoy the beauty of life once again. And so life goes, sometimes turbulent, but always followed by calm.

In between times of turbulence and calm, life often represents a free flowing of water, not turbulent, not calm; simply flowing along. It was 2000, and life was like that. Business was good. The family was healthy. Our life together was moving along in a somewhat "normal" fashion.

Then came another set of white water rapids. Emily, my thirteen-year-old daughter, attempted suicide. Emily's first mental health crisis crashed down upon our family and we were back in the white water rapids all over again.

Life is like that stream. The rapids seem to appear more frequently closer to the headwaters, and the speed with which the water flows can be frantic. As the water moves on toward the sea, the stream becomes broader and deeper; the rapids, when they appear, are of greater force; yet the deep slow moving pools of water allow a much-needed break in the action.

As the waters become deeper and broader, so likewise, with experience, do our lives. They call it wisdom. I call it a well of relief, knowing that there are more rapids lying ahead, just around the bend.

What you do between these periods of turbulence greatly affects your ability to "ride the rapids" safely. Knowing that life is filled with challenging experiences should cause us to want to prepare. But, if you are like me, you simply ride each set of rapids, hoping that the end is just around the bend. That's how I was for a full year after Emily's first psychiatric hospitalization. I was overwhelmed by the rapids and there was no bend in sight. I needed help.

It was at this point that I discovered "duct tape" and "WD-40".

Now what exactly is "duct tape" and "WD-40"?

Duct tape will be a different thing for each person, but for me it is focused prayer. You might use it as quiet reflection, time alone, time spent talking with a significant person or just pondering what to do next. The purpose is to get beyond yourself so you can see more clearly. Whatever your duct tape is it will have to be used daily to be effective.

On the other hand WD-40 is about listening. I find that listening to others takes the focus off of myself and frees me to be more caring. You need to make yourself completely available to another in terms of time and attention.

Chapter 2 will tell you more about these two essentials for quality living. Chapters 8 and 9 will go into the specifics of how to do it.

God told me to write this book. Why? I didn't know myself for the longest time. I simply responded as I felt called, and started to write. Then, as the calm of life set in once again, and I could take a normal breath, the answer came loud and clear:

More than anything, I want to work with people who are faced with the unpredictable and often frustrating behaviors of a loved one who suffers from a mental illness. I want to help them to:

- Accept that their loved one suffers from a mental illness.

- Understand that a mental illness, like other illnesses, is treatable.

- Believe that there is hope for recovery.

- Realize that they can make a difference in that recovery.

- Want to learn what it is they can do to help.

I have come to realize that there are millions of people just like me; people who are moving along the river of life believing that everything is under control. Then, without warning, they get a phone call telling them that a loved one is in the hospital, having attempted suicide, and their "white water rapids" pull them under and down so fast, they find it impossible to breathe.

From my first encounter with Emily's mental illness, I spent a year hiding from the reality that surrounded me. Then I surfaced to once again face life as it was. It is my hope that you will surface much sooner than I did and that you will learn to use your own version of duct tape and WD-40 to help you live a purpose filled life once again.

Won't you join me on this journey through life's rapids and toward calm flowing waters?

Now, let me tell you more about my Emily.

Chapter 1

"MY EMILY"

My journey into the darkest corner of hell began on that fateful day in May of 2000. It began as I sat in my car enjoying my second cup of coffee. I was hurled into the darkness by a voice, my wife's voice. Her message had been left on my cell phone.

"Wherever you are hon, pull over," my wife, Rob, said on the voice mail message. "I have some bad news for you."

Pull over? I hadn't even started the car. Bad news? I had been braced for something bad because of the first voice mail from a neighbor. But it had been vague and my mind was swirling as I attempted to piece together bits of information. Besides, we always search for some non-threatening explanation. Maybe, just maybe it was someone else's bad news. It's called denial.

Rob's voice cut through my spinning thoughts like a well-honed straight razor.

I noticed for the first time that the sky was overcast, almost gloomy. I realized that something terrible, unspeakable, hung on my wife's words. It had only been a fraction of a second after her first words, but it seemed like an eternity waiting for what she had said next. With my stomach spewing acid, fear was rising up to form a steel shank in my chest; I held my breath waiting for the message. Dreading what was to come!

Then it came, "Emily is at the Hershey Medical Center. She attempted suicide this morning."

Emily? My thirteen-year-old daughter? My baby? My God!!!

The message continued, "Emily had apparently overdosed on medication and then called 911. Don't worry. They say she'll be fine. I'm on my way there now."

"Don't worry? She'll be fine!" I was piecing this together with the only other information I had. The first voice mail had been left by a neighbor, saying Emily had come home from school that morning, crying, and that later an ambulance had been parked in front of our house. My mind had raced through the possibilities!

I was numb by now. There's no way to describe the fear, the confusion, the panic, the racing thoughts. Even today it is so difficult to recall.

Hit by a ton of bricks doesn't even come close.

Then it got worse. The last part of the message was, "Don't worry, Hon," Rob said, "It's not your fault."

My fault? What the hell was she talking about? My wife had just told me my daughter's attempted suicide was not my fault. My fault. The words fired off repeatedly in my head as I raced toward the hospital, about a half hour's drive away. I'm sure I made it in twenty minutes, maybe less.

Of course this wasn't my fault – but wait. A few weeks ago, at the dinner table I had screamed at Emily. I mean screamed. I swore she had lied to me and if there is one thing in life I will not tolerate, it is being lied to, especially by my teenage daughter. We fought so loudly I'm surprised the neighbors hadn't called the police. Finally, Emily left the table and went to her room. I "won."

I replayed that scene over and over again, as I raced the miles to the Hershey Hospital. I won. Why? Because I intimidated my daughter to the point of submission?

On the way to the hospital's emergency room, I saw a woman I knew. She came up and wanted to talk. I flew right past her. I think I told her my daughter had attempted suicide. It's all a blur now. When I arrived at Em's room I quickly found that they were right. Emily was OK physically. She had been given whatever they give people who overdose on meds and she was lying on her back...smiling. My Emily was going to be OK. I remember hugging her, but not much else.

I only have this vague memory of my conversation with Emily. I'm sure I made a joke or two. My tendency in a crisis is typically to offer distractions, to find some humor. In this case, though, I can't swear to it.

I remember two school officials showing up at the ER. Kids apparently had told them Emily was upset and had left school. They must have come with the police. The police and these two folks from school had searched my house, an unsettling thought, but an understandable one given the situation that they faced.

I would learn later that there was a suicide note. It had been left on her computer screen. Emily had come home and written it that morning.

It expressed anger with her middle school friends. In it, she reassured mom and dad, she was not angry with us, in fact she loved us.

I assumed Emily would now be discharged to go home with us. No! The psychiatrist came in and told us what would happen. Emily would be committed to a psychiatric hospital for at least three days. An ambulance was on its way to pick her up and take her there. No, we couldn't take her. No, she couldn't go home with us. She had to go to the psychiatric hospital. Something about it being a state law. I don't remember. I was angry, confused, lost...bitter!

I stayed that way for more than a year.

I call that day "My Emily." Most of us who have lived long enough have had at least one. Many younger people think they have had one. Some of us think we have had more than one.

That day, May 18, 2000, was mine. It was a day that would change my life, forever.

This book is about how I climbed out of the depths of hell. It took more than a year before I began the climb, and I'm still climbing today. This is about my spiritual journey, Emily's courage, and my family's efforts to recover.

But this book is also about you.

God told me to write this book. To write it for you and people like you who have, are, or will experience that day I have called "My Emily." That may sound crazy to some of you, never the less, I know it with my heart and with every fiber of my being. OK, you can be skeptical and that's fine. But consider this, what if this book really is for you? Could you afford not to continue reading?

When your day comes – not *if*, but *when* – this book will help you deal with it. No matter the cause, whether it's the death of a loved one, losing your job, a bitter divorce, or another type of personal crisis, you will experience your "Emily." When it happens, you need to know that there is help if you want it and are willing to accept it. That there are individuals and experiences that will help pull you out from those now unimagined depths.

No matter when you have your "Emily" – your severest time of need – I hope that what I've learned will help you to prepare for facing that day. I learned the hard way. It doesn't need to be that hard for you. Help is at hand. And that's what I want – no, what I've been told – to share with you.

I am fifty-eight years old and my name is David Anderson Brown. I am a father, a husband, a son, a brother. I am self-employed. I'm a man of faith! I am a volunteer. I'm a person who always said, "Yes" until the day my world collapsed in upon me. I am a person very much like you.

I am also a storyteller because I have learned that some of life's greatest lessons are to be found in stories.

What I learned has been working for me. I learned that along with life comes pain. Experience defines pain. Pain brings wisdom. Only when you acknowledge that the pain of where you are is greater than the pain of where you want to be, will you seek to change. Each of us need not deal with our pain alone. There is help available to us. We need to be aware of that fact and be willing to avail ourselves of it. I was in a world of pain. I needed help and I finally got it.

Chapter 2

USING NEW TOOLS

When God called out "tools," I thought he called for "fools," so I turned and went the other way.

Okay, it's an old joke. Forgive me. But I need to communicate just how inept I am when it comes to doing anything that smacks of "handyman" efforts. My parents bought me a simple toolbox when I left home the first time. I still have it, but I still haven't used all the tools that are in it.

I have gone on several mission work trips with our church, not because I have any interest or ability in the physical work that is done, but because Emily wanted to go the summer of her suicide attempt. I would do anything to support Em in her recovery.

I discovered there was one part of home improvement that I enjoyed: I love tearing down that which needs to be replaced. Give me a rotten deck and a claw hammer, and I'm your man.

We bought a home in 1975. We still live there, more than thirty years later. The house was built in 1912, and has a Victorian flavor. We bought it because of all the natural hardwood features: pocket doors between the parlor and foyer, open staircase with wood banister, hardwood floors…at least the parts that we saw. The day we move in we discovered that the hardwood floors were only hardwood around the perimeter. The soft, unfinished centers had been covered with area rugs, which were now gone, taken by the previous owner. However, it was a home with potential…it still is if you know what I mean.

Having been married for less than a year, I was a young man, filled with good intentions. I knew that I was not a "gifted" handyman, but I also knew that I couldn't afford to hire anyone. By the end of this story you will better understand why my wife established a rule: "I'm not to fix anything around the house." My job is to earn enough money to pay for someone to fix things around the house. That's why our home is still a home of potential.

The wallpaper in every room was ancient. We knew that we had to replace it. However, we decided to do it one room at a time, starting with the smallest bedroom which would be our nursery…another story in and of itself.

This small room had one of the four walls covered with a piece of wood paneling, which didn't look right at all. One giant rip and the panel was lying on the floor. We suddenly knew why the panel was there. It was there to hide a gaping hole in the horsehair plaster.

I like a challenge. Always have; always will. My challenge was to repair this hole and then wallpaper the whole room. I called a friend, who did this type of work all the time. He gave me a list of supplies I would need, and suggested that I get the Reader's Digest Home Repair Book.

Home Depot wasn't even an idea back then, so I ended up at the local hardware store owned by a neighbor just two doors away. He was more than happy to supply me with everything I needed and to open up an account so that I could pay the bill over a few months rather than all of it up front.

I started the job that evening and worked at it diligently for several evenings. I cut drywall to fit the hole. I taped the dry wall. I used a trowel, and drywall cement. I sanded. I repeated the whole process at least three times before I felt as if the job was nearly perfect. This is so unlike me, but I wanted to please my wife, and I wanted to experience some sense of satisfaction having met the challenge.

The repair was done. The wallpaper went up. The room was cleaned. The furniture was moved back, including a floor lamp, which I placed in the corner by the wall I just repaired. I opened a cold beer in celebration while I waited for my wife to get home. She arrived. It is now dark outside. I call her upstairs. I tell her to close her eyes and stand in the doorway. I turned on the floor lamp. She opened her eyes and began to laugh. That's not quite the reaction I expected. I looked at where she was staring, which was the wall that I had repaired. With the light shining brightly, there, in all its glory, was the shadow giving evidence to my lack of perfection. You could see quite clearly, the outline of the hole. I wanted to cry. Instead, I moved the light. The shadow was gone. Problem solved.

It was experiences like this that led me to discover the practicality of duct tape and WD-40. I always have a roll of duct tape on hand: the rule is "If it moves and it shouldn't, use duct tape." Duct tape has for years served as a great tool, providing temporary relief from an annoying problem until a more permanent solution can be found.

Likewise, I learned to use WD-40 years ago at my hunting camp. The rule is, "If it doesn't move and it should, use WD-40." Like its counterpart, WD-40 has helped me solve numerous household problems with a simple push on its spray applicator.

I'm taking the liberty of applying these simple tool concepts to the more human problems of life. When I was so overwhelmed with "my Emily," it felt as if I was falling apart. Hence, I had a need for duct tape of some sort. Later, I discovered that a year of denial caused many of my close personal relationships to be stuck. Remember? If it's stuck and it shouldn't be? You got it! WD-40. I needed to find some way of renewing those relationships.

After "My Emily," my thoughts were moving uncontrollably at times. Having lost my focus resulted in the loss of business, friends, family… they hadn't moved. I had moved. They were all still there, but I couldn't reach them through my pain.

God? Yeah, right! I was so angry with the Almighty that I gave the Supreme Being the cold shoulder. If you are married, you know this expression well. You can be so angry with your spouse that you choose to ignore one another. When you are really, really, angry you sleep so close to the edge of the bed it's a wonder you don't fall out. Well, that's how angry I was with God. I ignored God for about a year.

When I finally got around to asking God, "Why me?" his response was, "Why not you! What makes you so special that you shouldn't have to bear some tragedy in your life? Do you think you are the only one with a problem? Get over it, Brown. It's time to move forward."

That was a rather rude awakening! I looked around. God was right. I still had my health, my family, my business, and my friends. Why did I feel so alone? I thought I was abandoned but in reality no one had moved away from me. I was the one who had built a wall that shut everyone and everything out. God never moved away from me. I was the one who needed duct tape in a bad way.

This book is filled with stories to which hopefully you can relate. Most of them are my stories. The reason we tell stories is to remember. Every story has a point for someone. If I have done my job right, you'll laugh at some, cry at others. The crying is the most helpful. Why? If you don't hurt enough to cry, you won't do anything to heal the pain. It's one of those strange things about the human condition.

My wife taught me that lesson many years ago. I came home from work one day complaining about everything. For every complaint I had, she offered a solution. For every solution she offered, I had a reason why it wouldn't work. Finally, she simply said, "I see. You're not ready for a solution yet. You are still angry and you are not ready to give up your anger."

If you are still angry and not ready to give up that anger, you will read this book with someone else in mind. You might be entertained but the book won't do you much good. This book is for you. In fact, you are in this book and as you continue to read you will find yourself again and again.

We'll start with duct tape strategies to hold you together until you learn how to focus once again. When you're back in control of yourself – when you've regained your emotional security – you will be ready to deal with the ones you love, the ones you have most likely hurt.

Then we'll pick up the WD-40 and show you how to unfreeze relationships that are stuck. Listening to others works to accomplish just that. Your being there for others more than just for yourself, requires a lot of WD-40 because it is so easy to forget and focus back on yourself.

If you're an impatient soul, like me, you'll find this recommended process is extremely slow and seemingly unproductive. That's just a feeling. Get over it. If you want to regain control over your life, you can't keep doing what you have been doing. That will only get you more of what you already got. Trust me on this one, especially. Einstein defined insanity as doing something the same way over and over again and expecting different results. You have to do things differently. It's time to use duct tape and WD-40.

It was the day after Emily's suicide attempt, and I was in the white water rapids of life again. I needed something to hold me together long enough so that I wouldn't drown. I had no idea what it was at the time. I simply knew I needed something. I was broken and the only tool that was handy was duct tape.

WD-40? Where did that come from? "If it doesn't move and it should… use WD-40." I was stuck, too. My relationship with Emily was stuck. My marriage was stuck. My business was stuck. Everything in my life was at a standstill or moving backward. I needed something. I didn't know how that would look. I simply knew I needed help in all of my relationships. If you use WD-40 to unstick things, maybe it would unstick me.

Chapter 3

A HARD LESSON TO LEARN

Rejoice and be glad? You've got to be kidding! Not on May 18, 2000.

That day is as vivid a memory for me, as September 11, 2001. It is forever embedded in my mind and heart.

Rob went to the psychiatric hospital to be with Emily. I went back to my home town, Camp Hill, to take care of our daughter Susan, then eleven years old.

Susan knew nothing of what had occurred. As I drove to her middle school my dread continued to build mile by mile. How do you tell your daughter her older sister tried to kill herself? I didn't have a clue.

The principal had been kind enough to set up a conference room. It was as difficult as anything I faced that day. Somehow, I told Susan and somehow we coped. The rest of the day was a blur. The two of us spent time together at the house where just that morning Emily had overdosed on a meds cocktail.

I remember one thing. I started drinking that night. I'm not proud to say it but that's what happened.

"I understand you have a bad temper" was one of the first statements posed to me by this young social worker, or whatever title they gave her. Look, she was doing her job. However, it just hit me the wrong way. After all, this was about Emily, and not about me.

We were in a small room; Emily, my wife, this social whatever-worker, and me. A couple of days had passed and this was the first of several "conferences" the hospital insisted we attend.

"Emily tells me you have quite a temper, at times, Mr. Brown. Is that true?" I looked at Emily and she stuck her tongue out at me. Whatever trust Em and I shared with one another, from that moment on it disappeared. Internally, I began to boil.

"Temper? She thinks I have a temper!"

I was so angry and upset that I was ready to prove the correctness of her statement. Fortunately, common sense prevailed.

To those who know me it may come as a shock that I have a bad temper. I'm often described as "laid back, quiet, reserved." I learned at an early age that when I lost my temper I would say things that were hurtful. I was a master at verbally annihilating someone, usually someone I loved. Then, I never got what it was I really wanted. Usually, when I lost my temper I got more of what I didn't want. Therefore, I became a master at hiding my temper – taking it with me for a long walk instead.

Those long walks were on a good day. On a not so good day, I'd pour a Manhattan. I would rationalize that I never drank to become drunk. I'd have one or two to "take the edge off." It never really helped. Often, it made matters worse.

I thought that losing my temper once in awhile with my kids was justi-fied. They needed to know right from wrong. They needed to know when they fell short of their potential. It's all part of a father's job, isn't it?

We would eventually learn that what we were dealing with was bipolar disorder. They called it a mental disorder. I called it an excuse for Emily's aberrant behavior. Call it what you want, it's what they told us Emily suffered from. The good news was that there was medication to treat the problem. Great! Problem solved.

What they didn't tell you was that your life would never be the same. What I didn't realize then was that I needed to make major changes. That was just as important as Emily getting treatment. I had a long, long way to go.

Many of you may be asking the question, "What is bipolar disorder?" I didn't know much about this illness myself until 1988, the year that my daughter, Susan, was born. It was also the year that my mother-in-law, Kit, was diagnosed with bipolar disorder.

Bipolar is a mental disorder that had been known as manic depres-sion. It is caused by a chemical imbalance in the brain. Untreated, the mind operates from one of two "poles." The mania behavior looks like the person has a never-ending source of energy. Their thoughts are faster than normal individuals, often leaping from one subject to another. They often have grandiose ideas. They can be either exception-ally happy or quite irritable, making it very difficult to communicate with them.

Depressed behavior is just the opposite. A person who is depressed has very little energy. They often stop doing things that used to give them great pleasure. They are overcome with feelings of helplessness and hopelessness.

In Emily's case, her moods would cycle back and forth, changing from day to day, sometimes hour to hour. They would tell us that her bipolar disorder was of the rapid cycle type.

The depressed behaviors were easy to see. There were mornings that Emily simply refused to get out of bed, let alone get ready to go to school. On days that she did go to school, she would come home, retreat to her bedroom, and sleep. She no longer participated in many of the things she used to do that were fun. She stopped seeing the friends that she had made through school. She simply escaped into her own secret world.

She used to clip pictures of sad faces out of magazines and tape them to the walls of her room. Using red ink, she would color tears onto these faces. I later learned that this was to reflect her hidden pain.

Yes, we did take her to a therapist. Yes, we did have her treated with an antidepressant drug. None of this seemed to have much of an effect. That's because her diagnosis was wrong. We didn't see the positive behaviors for what they were…mania.

A day or two later, not only would she be eager to "seize the day," her energy level was over the top. For example, one spring day she asked if we could start a garden in the backyard. I reluctantly said yes, thinking about all the work that I would do that would soon go unnoticed. If Em wanted it, I'd do it. That afternoon, Em came home from school and in less than an hour had turned over seventy-five square feet of top soil…a task that would have taken me half a day.

Another example was the afternoon she cleaned our basement. Our home stands on a mountain stone foundation. The basement is unfinished, used primarily for our laundry room and the storage of "stuff" that is too big to store anywhere else, and no one has the courage to throw in the trash. Em wanted another space in the house she could call her own. With that as her goal, she moved everything around creating a "nest" so to speak in the corner, complete with a claw footed tub left over from the old bathroom, lined with blankets and pillows.

Another sign of mania was the rapid speech. She would talk so fast that it was often difficult to follow her train of thought.

These behaviors, although out of the norm, were a welcome relief from the "doom and gloom" of depression. It was not easy to see them for what they were; symptoms of bipolar disorder.

Untreated, this illness can have a profound affect upon the person who suffers and those who live with them. My anger was a direct reflection of my lack of understanding. I did not realize that my daughter was mentally ill. I still thought that she would respond to logical arguments and punishment for inappropriate behaviors.

Because there are many families living with someone who suffers from a mental disorder, I feel compelled to be very open with what happened to my life as a result of Emily's illness. Emily, too, is very open about her illness. We both realize that there is hope for recovery. We both want to help others.

My friend and mentor, Charlie "Tremendous" Jones taught me, in order to make a point, tell a story! And, my Dad was a great storyteller. So, I guess that's where I picked up the habit of telling stories myself. The point of this one is significant to our journey.

Now, let me tell you a story.

"Did I ever tell you about my pet dog, Dempsey?" my dad asked.

Dempsey was sort of a police dog who loved horseflies.

Dempsey would always follow Dad around the farm as Dad did his chores. In the summer he'd hunker down in the shade to wait for my dad. Dad said that, "Dempsey would sit still as a statue, waiting for horseflies to come close. As soon as one was close enough, Dempsey would snap it out of the air…just like a frog. No question about it," Dad said. "Dempsey loved horseflies."

"One summer day, my mom told me to get rid of the hornet nest that hung in a tree near to her clothesline. No problem! I got a long bamboo pole, a dried corncob, some wire, and kerosene. I soaked the corncob in the kerosene, and then wired the corncob onto the pole. I lit the corncob and began to move this long torch towards the hornet nest. Dempsey, as always, stood right by my side, watching my every move.

"Hornets are not stupid! They post guards outside their nests at all times. The guards sent word that their nest was under attack, and the swarm moved out immediately. Knowing the pain associated with a hornet sting, I dropped the pole and ran towards the pond. Dempsey chose not to follow. He apparently thought that this swarm would make quite a banquet. As I looked over my shoulder I saw Dempsey snap at the whole swarm, taking as many as he could into his mouth.

"I don't remember ever seeing Dempsey run as fast as I saw him run that day. He raced around the house, through my mom's clean clothes, pulling the clothesline along behind him. Off he went through the barn and the chicken coop, yelping all the way. Then he took off for the neighbor's farm, behaving much the same way. Dempsey disappeared, not to be seen again for a couple of days. We thought he went off somewhere to die, but good old Dempsey came limping back to the farm, his face swollen to the size of a full-grown pumpkin.

"It took several days before Dempsey began to look and act normal. As time went on, old Dempsey seemed as good as new except for one thing. He'd still follow me around the farm as I did my chores. He'd still hunker down in the shade. But, he never ate another horsefly the rest of his life. I guess he never forgot the pain associated with that swarm of hornets. Every flying insect reminded him of hornets. So, unfortunately, he stopped doing the very thing that at one time had given him so much pleasure."

My dad told me that story one day after he noticed that I was hesitating to take action on an important decision. I was considering starting my own business, but was scared to death of sales. Dad remembered my one bad selling experience. I had been trying to earn a few extra dollars during my college years by selling encyclopedias, when one potential customer literally threw me off his porch. The next day I turned my sales kit into my sales manager, vowing never to sell again. Dad's story helped me to see that my reluctance to act was based upon an old fear. Like Dempsey, I had concluded that the entire sales profession was like a swarm of hornets. Unlike Dempsey, I now knew the difference. With that realization, I was ready to act by taking my first step into what has turned out to be a lifelong career.

Twenty-five years later, I was faced with another mouthful of hornets. This time they were the memories of my Emily, sticking her tongue out at me. I was so bothered by her distrust of me that I stopped doing all the good things we used to do together. We barely even talked with one another except in polite ways at the dinner table.

It took a whole year before I was willing to admit that I was simply reacting to a hornet sting. It was only after I admitted it that I was able to even consider doing anything about it. My behavior did nothing to contribute to Emily's recovery. If anything, my distancing behavior hindered Emily's recovery.

What had moved? I had! I distanced myself! If it moves and it shouldn't, what's required?

Duct tape.

But, I didn't know that yet either.

Chapter 4

SURROUNDED BY LOST DREAMS

Denial is something that everyone else can see except for the one who is in it.

How can you not know you are in denial?

Not only can't you see it when you are in it, you don't believe it when people tell you. What I do know is that I used to dream dreams, but by this time, I had lost all hope. My dreams disappeared, and I didn't even know it.

"Denial? Me? I don't think so!"

The next few months were nothing more than a blur. Summer was almost here which meant that the forums, which I facilitate, were going into their normal summer break. That was good, because I was so distracted by what happened to Emily that I welcomed the break from business as usual. The only problem was I didn't realize then that this summer break would extend into next summer.

The next school year was a nightmare for all of us. I can't imagine what it was like for Em. She was the one who had to go back and face her classmates and her teachers. Ours is a small school district, less than

700 students in K-12, which means that everyone knows everything about everybody, or so it seems.

It wasn't long before Emily started to skip school. I hated waking her up on school days because odds were she would say she was sick and wanted to stay home. Here is where a huge battle was taking place in my own mind. Up until this time the rule was if you weren't bleeding profusely, your temperature was below 101 degrees, and you had no broken bones, you were going to school. Well, the rules changed without my knowing it. Em's mom was sympathetic to Em's emotional state far more than I was. Together, they would convince me that it was in Em's best interest if she stayed home.

This went against everything I believed. Not only that, I felt obligated to stop doing what it was I was doing at work so that I could go home and make sure Em was safe. Business suffered because my brain was not in the game. I suffered because I was embarrassed by my daughter's increased absences from school and her poor grades. Who was this person living in my daughter's body? What happened to my Emily?

Emily always was a charmer. She had a gift for language far beyond her years. The fact that she spent so much time in the adult world, observing life with her uncle inside the beltway of Washington, D.C., gave her ample opportunity to refine her persuasive abilities.

Who is Emily's uncle? In the family he is known as Uncle Newt. The rest of the country knows him as "Newt." Newt Gingrich is Rob's brother, hence my brother-in-law.

To give you an idea of just how persuasive Em could be, let me tell you about the night she was confronted by the U.S. Capitol Police. As a family, we were visiting her Uncle Newt in his office, which was right off the capital rotunda. Emily was in sixth grade at the time. Susan was in fourth. When evening came, and the work of the day ended, we all gathered in Newt's office for "adult conversation." Emily, and her sister, Susan, not wanting to be a part of that, asked if they could leave the office and explore the capitol building. Please understand that they knew that building inside and out. They had been on so many tours that they knew more than most of the tour guides seemed to know. Since the building was closed to the public and secure with the presence of the U.S. Capitol Police, we gave them our blessings.

Within a few minutes, the girls were brought back to their uncle's office, told by the police that the building was now closed – even if they were the nieces of the Speaker of the House. The girls sat quietly while the adults talked, but it was obvious that Emily was scheming. She soon got up, walked over to her uncle's desk, took a large pad of yellow Post-it notes, a Sharpie, and began to write. Within a minute she was done, walked over to her Uncle Newt, handed him the Post-it notes and the Sharpie, and asked him to sign it. Tears of laughter rolled down his cheeks as he quickly signed the note, peeled it off the pad and placed it on Emily's blouse, and off she and Susan went.

What Em had written was *"We have permission to roam the capitol. – signed, Newt Gingrich, Speaker of the House."*

The girls were gone for an hour, using their imaginations as they explored the capitol in ways that tourists would only dream about. The Capitol Police kept them in their view at all times, but knew not to bring them back to the Speaker's office until the Speaker asked them to.

What happened to that wildly creative, bold and daring little girl? Where did she go? Who was it that was now living in her body? Why couldn't I have Emily back?

Em now took strange pleasure in shocking people. She would say things that were so bizarre people would stare at her in disbelief, not knowing how to react. "Did she just say what I thought she said?" was a common theme in the minds of many who talked with Em.

I was told that all of her current behaviors were symptomatic of this mental illness called bipolar. Mental illness? No way. My Emily had a mental disorder that would be fixed as soon as they found the right combination of medicines. Denial!

Home life wasn't much better. My wife and I were afraid to go out and leave Emily alone for fear of what she might do. I never knew whether Em was really okay, or whether she was hiding her pain from our view. Even though she tried to assure us that she was okay, the memory of her suicide attempt was so vivid that it clouded all of our thoughts. While I wasn't looking, fun had disappeared from our family.

Susan was the silent sufferer. I tried to maintain a normal father/daughter relationship with Suz. Tried and failed. Even though I spent time with Susan physically; mentally, I was worrying about her sister. Susan, being the most introspective one in the family, could see right through me. She seldom complained. She simply went about attempting to be the opposite of everything Emily was. Em was loud. Suz was quiet. Em listened to punk rock music. Susan would listen to Christian contemporary music and Broadway musicals. Em would dress in ways that would draw attention. Susan began to wear blue and white…her school colors. Emily would show her anger. Susan would hide hers.

I'd come home at the end of each day dreading what might happen next. It's not that I'm the kind of person that likes just being normal. Matter of fact, our family view on life could be expressed in a line from a song from "The Fantastic's"… "Please God, don't let me be normal!" That was yesterday. Today I'd be thankful for normal.

On Sundays, I'd sit in church and want to cry. Everywhere I looked there were happy families. Father's Day was unbearable. No one bothered to go to church with me that first year. I remember watching other dads with their kids, laughing and hugging. Did you ever try and worship God when you are so angry you can't even think straight?

Lost dreams! I was surrounded by "lost dreams."

Living in a small community, I knew that my family was a favorite topic of discussion over backyard fences. It was a safe bet that we were part of their conversation somewhere along the line.

"Did you hear about Emily Brown? They say she attempted suicide."

"You're kidding? I always thought she was a bit odd. People say she is skipping school all the time…"

"You're right! I don't understand her parents. How can they let her do the things she does? Don't they believe in discipline?"

"Did you see what she was wearing to school the other day? How can her parents let her dress the way she dresses?" "If you think she dresses funny, you'll never believe what she talks about… just the other day my daughter came home from school and told me that Emily declared herself to be bisexual. What will she say next?"

Life that first year after Emily's suicide attempt was one continuous nightmare… camouflaged with smiles and rationalizations. I became a master at hiding my embarrassment. I did everything I could to pretend that nothing changed. People would reassure me by telling me they were sure Emily was simply going through some hormonal change, which occurs in all teenagers. Yeah! That's it! She's simply going through the throws of growing up. So she's taking a different path right now. That's just because she has always had a need to be different. She'll soon grow out of this phase and everything will be all right.

Dreams? What dreams? They had started drifting away on May 18, 2000, and then just kept right on drifting. I never saw them go. They faded away under the shroud of denial. With their passing, I lost what little hope I still had.

Picture this. You have a daughter who is physically ill. You have no clue what the illness is. You just know she needs help immediately.

You go to the emergency room with your daughter. Four hours later, a doctor tells you that your daughter needs to be hospitalized, but not at this hospital. She needs to be moved to a hospital specializing in mental illnesses. Okay. What is her diagnosis? We don't know! If you don't know, then how do you know she needs to be moved to this other hospital? It's the law. Your daughter tried to hurt herself. The law requires her to be hospitalized for at least three days (not counting Saturdays and Sundays).

That's how the nightmare begins.

Then, when you finally see your daughter, you still are not told what her diagnosis is. However, you are made to feel as if her illness is definitely your fault. "We understand you have a bad temper, Mr. Brown."

The day your daughter is released is the day they finally tell you your child's diagnosis. It is a disease you know nothing about, and the medical personnel, when asked, shrugs and says, "We have referred her to a specialist. The specialist will answer your questions."

A month later, you finally meet the specialist. The specialist tells you that your child, who just turned fourteen, doesn't want you to know her condition. "The law requires that we honor her request."

Let me see if I understand this. My child suffers from an illness, which affects her ability to make appropriate decisions. Her judgment is negatively influenced. However, there is a law, which strips me, her father, from all information that would help me to help my daughter?

That's correct!

That's insane!

It may be, but it's the law!

The nightmare continues. No one from mental health services tells you there are things you can and should do that would help in the recovery process for your child. Why not? There's no code that they can use to file for reimbursement of family services. Therefore, even thought it would help immensely, you are not brought into the planning of services. Now, it's not just the law that keeps you out. It's the lack of a code!

Our mental health care system is failing…completely. The nightmare grows worse. Everything is stacked against the family. When will you wake up? When will life go back to where it was before this nightmare began?

Chapter 5

YOU NEED HELP, BUT DON'T KNOW IT

One of my early professional mentors was a man of great faith. I watched Bill deal with a family tragedy that was beyond my comprehension at the time. He was married and the father of three daughters. The youngest, an infant, was diagnosed with a rare dysfunction within her digestive system. No matter what the doctors tried, it was impossible for this tiny infant to retain the nourishment that her body demanded. I know that Bill and his wife searched and searched for a medical miracle, yet none was to be found. The little girl died. Through it all Bill never seemed to lose his faith.

About the same time, my own career took a turn in a slightly different direction and I lost track of this man. One of the sad realities of today's human condition is that it is too easy to lose track of one another. Changing priorities take us in different directions, and often to different parts of the country. But the memories of my early mentor stayed with me and continued to influence my decisions in a number of ways.

For example, Bill would make a point of scheduling overnight trips with each of his daughters, four times a year. He said, "If you don't schedule it, it won't happen." As a result, I would do the same thing with both Em and Suz. Our hunting camp became a favorite retreat. Sharing my love for the outdoors with each girl, separately and, on occasion, as a family became a part of my life.

Twenty-two years after Bill's daughter died came my crisis with Emily. I remember how much Bill had held on to his faith in his crisis, so it was only natural for me to want to trust in God, too. As the days turned into weeks, and the weeks into months, my faith dwindled, slowly at first and then more rapidly. The pain of lost dreams was taking its toll in my spiritual life. The more I hurt, the more distant I became from my creator. The more distant I became, the lonelier I became. The lonelier I became, the deeper my depression. I was in a downward spiral, out of control.

Intellectually, I knew I needed help. Emotionally, I was too angry to admit it. The angrier I became the further away I moved from others. The more I moved away from others, the more self centered I became.

It's like finding yourself in a pond of quicksand, with all of your friends looking on. They've offered everything they know to offer; yet, you constantly refuse their gestures. You are sinking, yet you still believe that you can get out of this mess on your own.

Don't you just love the human spirit?

When there is something we want to do that we believe we shouldn't be doing, we can find some of the most creative reasons to justify our doing it. So I started smoking again. Smoking helped me relax. I enjoyed it. Surely, with all that I must deal with on a day-to-day basis, I deserve the right to enjoy something, don't I? Besides, no one knew? I smoked in the basement so as to not pollute my children's air. I didn't smoke in public, so clients and friends wouldn't know. It was just another little secret that somehow made me feel better.

Drinking! Smoking! And, I had also stopped exercising. I ended all of my volunteer work with the YMCA, an organization I truly loved. I stayed home every night and watched TV. I'd get up and go to work each morning only to move papers around or play solitaire on the computer. I didn't make any calls to anyone…customers, prospects, friends, family.

I paid a price for my less than healthy behaviors. I was experiencing slight chest pains. I failed the nuclear stress test. On February 1, 2002 I had a visit to the heart cath lab. My cardiologist found and removed an 80% blockage in my left anterior descending artery, better known as the Widow Maker. Thank God, my life was spared.

Not long after that My wife Rob told me that I needed to talk to a professional. I hated the idea of paying someone to listen to me. Our church was in turmoil and without a pastor. There was no one there who would understand. Perhaps that's why I gave up hope on the God of my understanding.

Matter of fact, in hindsight, I was quite angry at my church.

Rob is a fifteen-year breast cancer survivor. When she had her mastectomy in 1991, our church poured out its love. We had meals provided to us. We had phone calls, cards, letters, flowers, and visits. We felt God's love through and through.

When Emily was first hospitalized in a psychiatric hospital, our associate pastor and youth minister visited her one time, yet made no effort to see Rob or me. There was only one person who went out of his way to comfort me. He was the head of our men's Sunday school class. He called later that summer and took me out to lunch. All he did was listen. That's all anyone had to do. But, he was the only one who did.

The white water rapids were crashing in on me and sucking me under. My world was crashing in all around me. I felt alone. Rob was right. I needed help. I finally relented and sought the help of a psychotherapist.

The first session was okay. He hardly said a word, giving me lots of opportunities to do a "brain dump." The second session I brought a problem to the table that I considered impossible to solve. My wife wanted to put Emily on birth control pills. It seems one of the symptoms of Bipolar Disorder is sexual promiscuity. My Emily could be sexually active? This went against every fiber of my being. I figured if I were this emotional about an issue, I needed help from an objective observer. My psychotherapist fit the bill…until he gave me the advice he gave me. "It seems to me that you do what you don't want to do today, and put her on birth control; or risk a greater, more painful decision in the future."

I knew what he was saying was right. I just hated hearing it. I only went back to him one more time.

There are a few advantages to being in your mid-fifties: I get to go to the movies for $2.00 less than my wife, and I get to take advantage of the "senior specials" at restaurants.

Then there are other things that happen that aren't so great. Upon buying a new mobile phone last week, I asked the sales clerk what I could do with my old mobile phone. "You can give it to your grandchildren. It makes a great toy." she replied. Grandchildren? She actually thought that I looked old enough to have grandchildren? I am old enough. I just didn't want to hear it from someone else.

I attended college in the sixties, before the avalanche of change that has become such a huge part of our everyday life. My major was psychology. Most of what we learned had been well established in theory over several decades. In other words, we didn't have to worry that what we were learning would soon be displaced by something newer and more exciting.

Take Maslow's Hierarchy (see chart) for example. Abraham Maslow developed his model of human motivation earlier in the twentieth century. It was easy to understand and was therefore accepted by many in the human behavioral discipline.

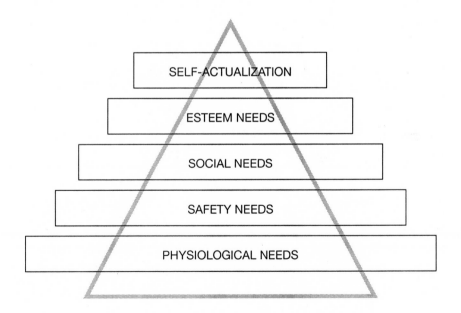

I'm sure that some of the newer models could explain the mysteries of my bizarre responses to Emily's bipolar disorder and all the strange and unpredictable events that happened as a result of Em's mental illness. However, Maslow's Hierarchy is so basic, that I didn't need to look anywhere else to gain an understanding of what had happened to me.

Why was it that I was frozen in the state of denial? Why couldn't I see what was happening to me? Why was I unable to hear what people were telling me?

In lay terms, Maslow's Hierarchy identifies five basic needs of human existence. Each one dependent upon the previous one being satisfied before a new one can be addressed. It starts with our basic **PHYSI-OLOGICAL** Needs, both physical and emotional. All of us have a need for food, clothing, and shelter. This basic need is what drives us to make sure there is something to eat each day, some place to sleep each night, and something to wear which will cover our nakedness and protect us from the elements.

The next level is that of **SAFETY**. Safety is what insures us that we not only have food, clothing, and shelter today, but we feel certain that we will have it tomorrow as well. Maslow's safety also includes emotions. Do we feel emotionally safe, and if so, do we believe we'll be emotionally safe tomorrow as well. If you are not sure of your wellbeing from day to day, then you are operating at the bottom of Maslow's Hierarchy, and that's not a fun place to be.

But suppose that your basic needs have been met and that you feel certain that those needs will be met tomorrow as well. If that's the case then you are now capable of working on the third level of needs, which are **SOCIAL NEEDS**. Social needs include our need to find and build close relationships. Love is the ultimate social need. When you find yourself in love, you feel as if nothing else matters in life.

Most people find that special relationship in life in their twenties allowing them to then focus on **ESTEEM NEEDS,** such as their next job promotion, challenging new project, service to the church, etc. The list of other things that fall in the area of accomplishment is endless and is only limited by our imagination.

Every once in awhile, we feel as if all things are going our way. We have the things we both want and need; we have a meaningful relationship with a significant other; we just got the promotion we had been working towards. Everything is as it should be and we feel on top of the world. This is what Maslow calls **SELF-ACTUALIZATION**. It seems that it seldom lasts very long because something comes along and knocks us down a rung or two, but it is unbelievable while it lasts.

"Life doesn't get much better than this!" is a slogan that describes what it's like to live life close to the top of the hierarchy.

Then you come home to an empty house, because your spouse moved out while you were at work. Perhaps you discover that your financial assets have declined rapidly due to some poor investment strategy. Or the doctor just told you that you have cancer and she's not sure how far along the cancer had progressed. What if a mental illness strikes someone you love, and strips them of characteristics that made them so special to you in the first place?

When you are hit between the eyes with such profound negative information you get tossed to the bottom of the hierarchy faster than you ever thought possible. All of a sudden your sense of security has been threatened. Your reaction is to detach yourself from everyone else while you try to figure out what happened. Worse yet, you enter into the world of denial and pretend that everything is okay, all while watching what is important to you in life slip away.

The river has once again moved you into the white water rapids. Life is overwhelming and you are drowning. You just can't figure out why you are behaving the way you are.

Yep! That was me! Drowning! At least I now understand why it feels as if I'm drowning. I was moving back down toward the bottom of Maslow's Hierarchy. I just hadn't figured out what to do about it.

Fortunately, I kept remembering what had been. It was those memories that kept me afloat while I continued my struggle for survival. "I can't drown. I'm not finished being a father."

Chapter 6

ADMIT THAT YOU HURT IN ORDER TO DO SOMETHING ABOUT IT!

Did you ever find yourself so instantly enraged that you said something that you immediately regretted?

My dad and I didn't fight very often. Perhaps that's why I can remember this particular one so clearly.

I was 17. I had been dating the same girl for several months. One day at breakfast Dad challenged me about dating the same girl for so long. He said that it was time for me to move on.

"Dad, the only thing you are afraid of is that I will get her pregnant. I'm old enough to know how a girl gets pregnant. I wouldn't risk that kind of behavior."

"Don't you talk back to me. Give me your car keys. You can drive again when I say you can."

Argument over!!!! Dad won. I tossed him my keys and stormed out of the house.

What caused my anger? Dad's judgment was unjustified. He only assumed that we were putting ourselves at risk. In the sixties, teen sex was not something that was talked about openly. Girls who became pregnant quietly disappeared from school. Rumors were rampant. But, no one talked about it openly.

I don't remember what happened the rest of that day until we were seated for dinner. Dad comes home, walks into the dining room and tosses me my keys. "You're right. You are old enough to accept responsibility for your behaviors. I trust you, although I still think you should date other girls."

Wow! Dad trusts me. Nothing more was said. I dated the same girl for three more years, and Dad never said another word. What had happened? What had caused him to change his mind?

I found out a few days later that Marie, my Dad's secretary of several years, had challenged his decision. Marie could have been my grandmother the way she took care of me. She always looked out for me – Dad, too. Dad had gone to work that day in a terrible mood. Marie knew he was upset by something, and had the courage to confront him as well as the gift of being able to help him reexamine his "rush to judgment." Marie asked what the problem was. He told her of our fight. Marie helped him see the situation from a different perspective. Dad changed his mind and "tossed me the keys." He changed his perspective in a day. It took me more than a year to change mine with respect to Emily.

Why? I wish I knew. I seldom wish that I could live any portion of my life over again. That year after Emily's suicide attempt is one that I wish I could.

So what changed my perspective? What allowed me to look at what happened differently? If Marie was the cause of my Dad's significant emotional experience which changed his perspective, what was mine? And what is yours?

This is not an ad for Promise Keepers, but it was that experience that changed my perspective. It will be different for each of you. Marie was my dad's significant emotional experience. She helped him see what had happened between he and I from a different perspective. A speaker at a Promise Keepers' Rally did the same for me.

A friend asked if I would join him on a trip to Baltimore to a Promise Keepers rally. I went reluctantly. He was the only person from my church who went out of his way to befriend me after Emily's suicide attempt. I owed him big time. I couldn't say no.

What I was expecting and what I experienced were two totally different things. What I expected, because the press conditioned me to expect it, was to be in the midst of a sea of white male chauvinist pigs. What I experienced was the most orderly crowd of 14,000 men, most carrying a Bible, walking from all different directions to the civic arena at half past seven in the morning. This was in total contrast with what I was led to believe. When we got inside I was even more amazed at the politeness of the crowd.

The arena was fairly quiet, considering the number of men pouring into the place. There was a scriptural reference on the large screen suggesting that reading scripture would be a good way to prepare for the service to follow. I looked around and saw a majority of men doing just that, reading their Bibles in public. Go figure.

Without warning, the band started playing loudly, people were up out of their seats clapping and singing a song, which I had never heard before. I think I was the only one who did not know the songs. Everyone else was loudly belting out the words to one song after another. I was definitely feeling out of place.

Then the music stopped and someone started to speak. I'm a lousy listener. I speak for a living, so I'm very critical of other speakers. I judge how they are saying things rather than listen to what they are saying. I had already decided that I could do a better job than the man at the microphone. So why listen?

The speaker was followed by more music and then more speakers. I was beginning to feel a bit more at ease. Then someone spoke about the importance of prayer. I felt a wave of guilt for I hadn't had much to do with prayer since May 18, 2000. After all, it's difficult to talk with anyone that you are angry with, especially God. Yet, for whatever reason, I was drawn to listen to this man.

I knew that I was guilty of turning my back to God. I was listening because I hurt, because I had no one else to talk to who had a clue as to what my life had been like this past year. I listened because I was lonely. I continued to listen. Why? I don't know! I simply had to listen. This was my significant emotional experience. This was the first time that I finally let go of my anger and was able to look at what happened to Emily and our family from a different perspective.

As the speaker continued I began to knock down preconceived barriers. What would happen if I stopped reading the paper and read the Bible instead? Think about it. Every morning millions of people get up, have a cup of coffee and read the paper. I bet most are like me. They read things that do nothing but make them angry or sad. Isn't that a heck of a way to start a day? There's the television, too. I always get mad watching "Good Morning America" (this was before Fox and Friends made it to our cable system). I suddenly realized just how negative a way this was to start each day.

The more he talked, the more I listened. The more I listened, the more I was moved to agree. The more I agreed, the more I looked for ways to pray rather than reasons why I couldn't or shouldn't.

So started my journey back. I committed to an hour of prayer each day for the next thirty days…not for a lifetime, but for thirty days. I figured I could do anything for a month.

A little more than one year from the day that rocked my world, my day at that Promise Keepers rally proved to be a watershed experience. It was the day I admitted that I was wrong. It was the start of my climbing out of the gloom and moving toward where I needed to be to help Emily and to begin to stabilize our family. Miraculous things began to happen.

It takes a significant emotional experience to break through the filter of preconceived values and beliefs. Until that breakthrough, the filter through which you look at life will not allow you to see anything other than what you believe to be true. My "filter" told me that Emily was a child with a brilliant IQ. She had performed well in school before; therefore, she could perform well again. My role as her father was to hold her accountable to that standard, and demand that she work hard to achieve it. That's what I believed…until that day I learned differently.

The experiences, which allow us to let go of old perspectives and embrace new ones, always come unexpectedly. You can't plan one. You can't create one. They come in many ways. Mine was spiritual. My Dad's was a trusted employee. My Dad only took a day to see a different perspective. It took me a year. Why? I wish I knew. If you take the time to reexamine your own life, I'm sure you'll discover you, too, have had the same kind of experience. Once I changed my perspective … once I admitted that I was wrong, I felt enabled to do something about it.

Chapter 7

WHEN IT MOVES AND IT SHOULDN'T USE DUCT TAPE

There are many things in life that should not move. For example, if you are in a raft and going through turbulent waters you want your oars to stay right where they are, attached to the raft. Life is exactly the same if you want to survive.

I had made a commitment. I committed to an hour of prayer each day for thirty days. It was one of those commitments that, having not told my wife, would be easy to rationalize my way out, pretending that the whole commitment thing was just a dream of sorts. I've had lots of experience rationalizing things in life.

But this time, I had made a commitment to God, not to myself. I knew it was for only thirty days, and I can do most anything for thirty days. But how was I going to find an extra hour a day? It was easier than I thought. First, I didn't go out and get the morning paper which was one of the first steps in my morning rituals. Next, I wouldn't turn the TV on. I would make a pot of coffee. I figured coffee was one of God's creations, so why should He object to my having a cup while in prayer? Finally, I found a comfortable place to pray; I simply curled up in my favorite chair.

So what's the problem? Have you ever tried to pray for an hour? I soon discovered that the challenge facing me was somewhat daunting. I have a hard time talking with anyone for an hour, let alone the Almighty, whom I cannot see…or hear.

The first day after my commitment has arrived. I'm up and showered, downstairs making coffee, thinking all along, "just how does one pray for an hour?" I figured that reading scripture would be a good thing to do since prayer is a two way process. Scripture, from my understanding, is how God talks to us; but, reading scripture for an hour is cheating, at least from my point of view.

Coffee is ready. I pour a cup, sit down, pick up my Bible, read a few passages at random, look at the clock, and fifteen minutes had gone by. All right! I'm one quarter of the way home.

I closed my eyes and ran through all that I thought I should pray for, and then looked at the clock. Two minutes had gone by. In my understanding of prayer, I was finished. What was I to do with the remaining forty-three minutes?

How in the world does one pray for one hour?

I closed my eyes and prayed again. I opened my eyes and only another two minutes had passed. Forty-one minutes to go.

This is like trying to have a conversation with someone who doesn't say a word, someone who sits there with a poker face, giving you no clues whatsoever as to what they are thinking. This was hard work.

As I sat there, somewhat perturbed by the difficulty of the task, my eyes focused upon a school notebook at the end of the table. "What if

I were to write a letter to God? Would that be a form of prayer? And if so, what would I say?"

So I picked up a pen, opened the notebook, and began to write. By the time I was finished, far more than an hour had passed.

Now I want to talk about my duct tape, but before I do let me be very clear about one thing. The only credentials I have with respect to using duct tape is that I have used it everyday, day after day over the past several years. I don't know if I use it the right way or the wrong way. All I know is that I have never felt the sense of meaning and purpose in life as I do today.

That sense of meaning and purpose comes from three years of using a daily journal, my primary form of duct tape, in a focused, reflective manner. As of today, I have nine notebooks filled with personal reflections.

Keeping a journal has become as natural as breathing. Matter of fact, like breathing, it is how I have to begin each day. To do otherwise is like still being asleep.

This journey toward my learning how to use duct tape is best described by what we know as the "four stages of learning."

There are some very large psychological/educational terms for these stages: Unconscious incompetence; Conscious incompetence; Conscious competence and Unconscious competence.

Here in simple terms is our understanding of what all that means and an illustration of how it works.

Stage one is, *you don't know you don't know.* Think of a toddler who, as of yet, doesn't know how to tie his shoes. At first, he doesn't know he doesn't know.

Stage two is, *you now know you don't know.* Then one day he suddenly realizes he doesn't know how to tie his shoes and he wants to learn how. His teachable moment is at hand.

Stage three is, *you now know, but have to concentrate to keep doing it.* Learning how to tie shoes is a tedious process. The first several attempts are very deliberate, and often met with failure. However, the desire to tie his own shoes keeps him motivated. He knows he knows how, but he must think about it each time he does it.

The fourth stage is, *the learning has become a part of you and you just do it without your having to think about it.* Finally, he gets to the point where he doesn't even think about it anymore. He simply ties his shoes as if he had been doing it all his life.

There is the story of the little boy who learned how to tie his shoes and went in excitedly to show his mom. When he finished he suddenly broke into tears. His mother asked him why he was crying. His response, "Now that I know how to tie my shoes, I will have to do it for myself the rest of my life!"

Before Promise Keepers, the significant emotional experience that broke through my wall of denial, I didn't know I didn't know. Using my form of duct tape didn't mean a thing to me. Keeping a journal wasn't even a concept in my mind.

I realized for the first time in my life that when it comes to taking time to focus, to reflect each day on my purpose in life, I didn't know how, and now I wanted to learn.

The first few weeks were awkward. I knew I had to use some form of writing because that is what worked for me. There are other options that might work better for you, but for me it was writing. It just seemed logical to pick up a notebook and start to write about the things in life that seemed to be so out of control.

I'd write positive one-liners and short sentences. Each day I was very deliberate. I was on the move toward something that would make a difference in our family and in my life. Today, it is like breathing. I do it without thinking; it became essential to my life.

Enough about me, let's talk about you. Let's suppose that at this point you have broken through your wall of denial. Let's further suppose that you are ready to begin using some form of duct tape to move toward regaining control of your life.

If that is the case, here is a simple formula to guide you:

- Start with a spirit of thankfulness. There are always some things for which you can be thankful. A bright blue sky or a cup of hot coffee or that your car just passed inspection. These may be small things, but now you have a starting place. No matter how bleak things seem, you can still see some goodness. See things through the window of thankfulness, not the window of hurt, anger, frustration, or disappointment.

- Acknowledge that you are the problem. How can you work to minimize the number of things you do that are just in the way? No matter how small or seemingly trite your actions appear to you, what you say or do can be painful to others.

- Focus your thoughts on a vision of hope. My vision of hope was "living in an emotionally safe home; a home of peace and joy to which my family could return at the end of each day." Your hope is probably the opposite of what you have now. How would you describe it?

I would reflect on this vision of hope by asking three questions:

1. What am I doing that is helpful? Do I want to continue doing that?

2. What am I doing that is hurtful? Is it behavior I want to stop?

3. What haven't I thought of before that I can start doing to help make things better?

Reflecting on these questions brings things to mind. I write them down so that I can insert some into my daily "to do" list. This gave me a sense of getting my act together.

Next, let's talk about your form of duct tape. Remember, if it feels like you're falling apart or having a hard time staying focused on anything you need duct tape. If it seems as if you have more problems than you know what to do with, if you have a high need to be in control, and you feel out of control, duct tape is essential.

Don't be hung up on this thing called prayer. Duct tape for you may look different than duct tape does for me. Just as faith comes in all shapes, forms, and sizes, so does duct tape.

Until you discover your form of duct tape, I suggest that you start with what I found that worked:

- Get a spiral notebook.

- Set your alarm for a half hour earlier than usual. When the alarm goes off get up, get out of bed, get moving.

- Put on a pot of coffee, or heat water for tea. Okay, a Diet Coke will do, too. Whatever your morning beverage is, allow yourself that moment of enjoyment.

- Find someplace comfortable. Sit quietly. Everything else can wait.

- Now start writing! Write down the things for which you are thankful. Now write the things you tend to worry about. No order needed. Simply get this stuff out of your head. It will help reduce your anxiety almost immediately. Each day add to your list until you feel as if you have all your worries listed. Get them out of your head and onto paper where you can look at them and begin to focus.

- Wow! I bet you never knew just how much you tend to worry about, did you? Sort them if you like: spouse; children; money; job; health; extended family; business…

- Here's the point. Out of all the problems you have listed, what is the one problem that if you could deal with it, all the rest would be easier? *Mine was the chaotic home life that greeted me at the end of each day.*

- Now envision how you would like it to be. In writing, describe the opposite of how it is now. *Chaotic home life? The opposite would be an emotionally safe home; a home, which offers sanctuary, comfort, peace and joy.*

You have now successfully identified the issue upon which you need to focus every day, day after day.

To stay focused start each day by reviewing what you have written. Now, quietly reflect. As you begin to take control of your day, listen to what your mind begins to tell you. Capture those thoughts. See if a pattern begins to take shape. Finally, decide what's most important for that day and commit to doing something about it.

This is my heart and soul, my journal. This is my duct tape.

What happened after I started using Duct Tape was miraculous.

CHAPTER 8

FIND PEOPLE WHO UNDERSTAND

The mission I developed through my journaling was to create an emotionally safe home; a home to which we all can return at the end of the day to a sense of peace and joy.

To do this, I had to change the way I reacted to Emily's behaviors. In times of crisis I had to stop yelling ... stop demanding .... stop judging .... stop responding the way I had been. I had to quit my knee jerk behaviors. These were the behaviors that would drive Emily further and further from me. These were the behaviors that kept our home from being an emotionally safe place.

You may wonder why I responded with such non-productive behavior. To understand this about me, let me use the "whole Person" model, a model that seeks to explain human behaviors. Think of a person as an iceberg. You only see the tip of the person when you see outward behavior. The factors determining any individual's behaviors are buried far below the surface, not visible to anyone...even to the person who is puzzled by their own behavior.

Remembering back to my mother-in-law's psychotic experiences, I recall being shocked by some of the words that came out of her mouth.

This polite person was saying some of the most shocking things directly to people. What had happened?

Her psychiatrist offered this explanation. All of us have filters in our brains that keep us from saying the things we want to say, from doing the things we want to do, but believe we shouldn't. When we do say things we are ashamed of, or do things we know we shouldn't do, that's the exception. For a period of time, Kit's filters completely malfunctioned. She would see or hear things, misinterpret them, and then respond in some of the most embarrassing ways...embarrassing to us, her family, not to her.

Looking at the Iceberg model (see image), you will see that just below the surface are the thoughts and feelings dictating behaviors. Below the thoughts and feelings is the filter, "values and beliefs". At the bottom of the iceberg are your basic behavioral needs. You **may** have a basic need to control, a need for positive interaction with others, a need for security, a need for conscientiousness, or a combination of any of these needs. The point is that we all have basic needs. It is when those needs are not being met that the filter above occasionally malfunctions, allowing us to behave in ways we otherwise would not behave.

Every once in a while we experience significant emotional events that cause us to look at the world through a different set of glasses. The filter of values and beliefs is challenged. Think of 9/11/01. All of us were affected by that significant emotional event. All of us have had our values and beliefs challenged. Some have definitely changed how they look at the world.

May 18, 2000 was the day of my significant emotional experience. My filter...my beliefs and values.... were challenged. Things changed. I no longer trusted Emily. I couldn't trust that she wouldn't attempt suicide again. I couldn't trust her when she stayed home from school. I couldn't trust her when her grades began to fall. I couldn't trust her when she clung to her boyfriend, violating my belief that public displays of affection are inappropriate. My filter of trust was changed, letting my need for control to surface frequently. I became demanding with greater frequency. I took control of Em's medications making sure she would take her meds when she was supposed to take them. I began to insist that she improve her academic performance. The list goes on and on.

What I didn't realize at the time was that I was asking the impossible of Emily. A person suffering from a bipolar disorder cannot control their mood swings; they cannot control their behaviors in environments of high stress. Asking them to do so is akin to asking someone who is asthmatic to stop wheezing when they are in the middle of an attack. My filter was malfunctioning simply because I didn't know better. I truly believed I was being the father that I needed to be.

It wasn't until God answered my prayer by leading me to Promise Keepers that I realized that I had been operating in a state of denial. I was challenged, by a friend to take the course, Family to Family. It was then that I finally began to repair my damaged filter.

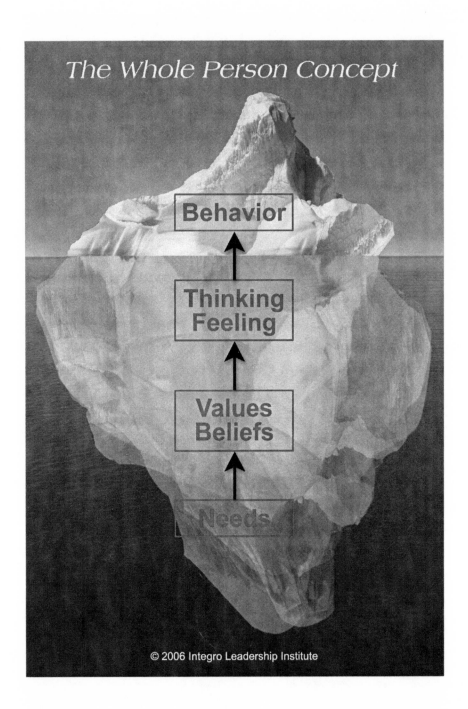

The Whole Person Concept

Behavior

Thinking
Feeling

Values
Beliefs

Needs

© 2006 Integro Leadership Institute

Perhaps that's where you are right now. Perhaps this book is your significant emotional event that causes you to stop and reexamine your values, your beliefs. Perhaps today is the day you want to begin to repair that filter.

I'm writing this chapter at the same time the people of New Orleans are struggling with their own significant emotional event, Hurricane Katrina. I'm watching helicopters dropping 3,000-pound bags of sand in the breaks of the levees in attempt to stop the flooding. What can you use to stop the flooding caused by your own malfunctioning filters?

My sandbags came in the form of a personal mantra: "Is this the mountain I want to die on?" This was the short-term fix, which kept me from saying the things that would trigger Emily's acting out. This was the phrase that I repeated to myself every time I would feel my need to control come bubbling up above the level of my filter, my values and my beliefs.

The long term fix was put in place the day I began to pray; pray every day, always writing my prayers, always writing my quest to "create a safe home emotionally, a home to which we can all return to at the end or each and every day in peace and joy." Every day that I prayed that prayer…. every day that I wrote it down… another strand was woven into the filter of my mind. Day after day, strand after strand. That's what it took to change the filter of my values, my beliefs and then eventually I no longer had to worry that I would respond inappropriately to those behaviors I had once believed to be intolerable.

People behave the way they behave because of what they think and feel. As a father, I knew that Emily had an exceptional IQ. Naturally, when her grades began to slide, I thought that my role was to hold her accountable for her performance, and to reason with her. Why did I think that? Because that is what I believed my role should be. That's how my father was, and he did a pretty good job.

When Emily did not meet my expectations, acting upon what I believed, I would allow my natural behaviors to surface, looking like someone trying to control a bad situation. My natural behavior is to be direct with people when problems surface. When I feel as if I'm not in control, directive behavior rapidly becomes demanding behavior. Demanding behavior often results in yelling. Because I believed that Emily was capable of better academic performance, and that my role was to hold her accountable, I saw little need to control my negative behaviors.

One of the things I desperately needed when I started this new journey was to find someone to talk to who understood what it was I was experiencing. I was tired of all the advice of well meaning friends who didn't have a clue what was going on inside of me. It was less painful for me to simply avoid them than to list to their ill-informed prattle. They were telling me:

"What do you mean, "She doesn't want to go to school"? No kid wants to go to school. Just make her go. Ground her if she doesn't!"

Now there's a thought. Ground her! But she doesn't go anywhere. How would it help to ground her? Oh, you mean punish her. Punish her! Why didn't I think of that? Been there, done that. Bought the T-shirt.

No one seemed to understand that Emily's school environment was so frightening that she would sooner kill herself then have to return to that dreadful experience day after day. Forcing Em to "get back on that horse" would be like killing her. It is as absurd as telling someone who suffers from fear of fire to run into a burning building to save a teddy bear.

People who suffer from a mental disorder cannot look at our world the same way you and I can. When emotions are so strong that logic is constantly overruled, logical arguments are a waste of time. All they do is serve to make both people angry and less trusting of one another.

I sat there in silent reflection, focused on my need; "God help me find someone I can talk with who knows what it is like to deal with the kind of life I'm dealing with." It was if God literally spoke to me, telling me that the answer was on the right hand corner of my desk. I got up and walked into the parlor…it is an antique desk that compliments our Victorian style parlor, or what we hoped would be a Victorian style parlor until Susan, my younger daughter, moved all of her guitars in and used it as her music lab…. and sure enough, there was a large envelope from someone who knows someone who knows us and knows of our current situation.

The envelope that I finally opened from NAMI: The National Alliance for Mental Illness was the start to finding the answers I so desperately sought.

When I read what NAMI did I felt the same uneasiness as I had before. Mental illness? My Emily? I don't think so. Em just has a "mental disorder". She's taking pills, lots of them, and she'll soon be better…or so I thought back then. Remember the chapter on denial? I was out of denial now. I didn't like it, but I was ready to accept it. My daughter suffered from a mental illness.

The person who sent this to me lived in Orange County in Southern California. They have a son who is a few years older than Emily, and suffers from Bipolar Disorder. I guess you can say they had some idea of what I was dealing with. We live in Central Pennsylvania and they were too far away to be helpful on a regular basis. I needed to see someone who lived close by.

Then I noticed the web address, www.nami.org. I'm not the most savvy techno kind of guy, but even I knew that there would be more information if I went to the web site. There it was: A link to NAMI PA, then a link to NAMI PA Cumberland and Perry Counties. It provided me with a name and contact information. I picked up the phone. I was on my way.

A week or two later, I found myself walking into a room full of strangers, who, by the time introductions were made, seemed like my new best friends. Everyone there had a loved one who suffered from some form of mental disorder: Bipolar Disorder, Schizophrenia, Schizoid Affective, and a handful of other disorders I never knew existed.

The moderator opened the meeting by reminding everyone about the rule: "what is said here stays here". I can't remember a thing about that first meeting, other than these were people who understood, and wanted to help. I felt such a sense of relief that evening. I wasn't the only person dealing with a mentally ill family member.

People asked questions, helping me clarify and prioritize my issues. A number of suggestions where tossed out for discussion. I don't recall what they were, nor is that important. What was important is that I found a group of people who understood what it was I was experiencing in my life and the life of my family.

A few days later I received a note of encouragement from one of the folks at that meeting. I didn't know that person, yet he took the time to write to me. Another person brought a book to the next meeting and gave it to me to read. She said that it had helped them when their son was hospitalized the first time.

Because the mental health industry has a void when it comes to being family friendly, NAMI was created. It is the nation's largest grassroots organization in the mental health field. It has been in existence for more than 25 years. Its membership is made up of "consumers" (people who suffer from a mental disorder), "family members" (people like me who love and live with someone who suffers from a mental disorder) and "providers" (mental health service providers). Their mission is very clear and compelling. "NAMI is dedicated to the eradication of mental illnesses and to the improvement of the quality of life of all whose lives are affected by these diseases." Their strategies are threefold: Education, Support, and Advocacy.

It was in the areas of education and support that I originally found the most benefit. It was a wonderful feeling to walk into a room full of people who knew first hand what life was like for me. I felt totally welcome at the first meeting I attended. These were people who had similar stories, similar experiences in life. A number of the group members were consumers who were dedicated to helping others better understand what their loved ones were probably experiencing. Most were family members, like me, who wanted desperately to make sense out of that which makes no sense ... the unpredictable and often frustrating behaviors of a loved one who suffers from a mental disorder. I quickly found myself looking forward to our affiliate's monthly meetings.

From a practical standpoint, the course, "Family to Family" was the most helpful. "Family to Family" has been proven to have an immediate and long lasting positive impact upon those who take the course. According to their web page, "The NAMI Family-to-Family Education Program is a free 12-week course for family caregivers of individuals with severe brain disorders (mental illnesses). The course is taught by trained family members who have experienced the same conflicts. All instruction and course materials are free for class participants.

The Family-to-Family curriculum focuses on schizophrenia, bipolar disorder (manic depression), clinical depression, panic disorder and obsessive-compulsive disorder (OCD). The course discusses the clinical treatment of these illnesses and teaches the knowledge and skills that family members need to cope more effectively.

Family-to-Family classes are offered in hundreds of communities across the country, in two Canadian provinces, and in Puerto Rico and Mexico."

Here in Pennsylvania, NAMI has been providing training for the law enforcement community. Too many consumers find themselves in trouble with "the law", and get caught within a system that offers them little help. If anything, the law enforcement community, unintentionally of course, makes matters worse. People who become a danger to themselves and to others due to a mental health crisis need to be hospitalized, not imprisoned.

If you are a caregiver for a family member suffering from a mental health disorder, please contact your local NAMI affiliate. For those of you wanting more information regarding NAMI (National Alliance for Mental Illnesses) visit their web page at http://www.nami.org/. You will find a wealth of information at your fingertips, as well as contact information regarding affiliate organizations.

The sad part of this story is that the mental health industry never told me about NAMI; in my case, there was little effort to involve the family in my daughter's recovery. I have since come to learn that I'm not all alone in this struggle. My story is a familiar one to thousands upon thousands of families across the country.

As I began to ask why the mental health system was not effective, the most common response I received was that there is insufficient funding. There is barely enough money available to treat the one who suffers, let alone the immediate family. Sure, they offered one or two ideas. But, there was never a sustained effort by any provider of mental health services towards the healing of the family. How can anyone expect someone who is mentally ill to have a chance to recover if there is no family willing and able to help?

Money was not a problem. Family-to-Family didn't cost me a cent, nor did it cost the providers a cent. It is a course that is taught by volunteers, by people who have been where the participant is now. They provided us with some helpful materials that were funded by both NAMI and our local MH/MR office.

Through this experience I came to some conclusions:

1. Recovery is possible.

2. Recovery requires an ongoing systemic process including the one who suffers, the mental health provider, and the family.

3. Volunteers through NAMI and their Family-to-Family course, thereby minimizing the financial impact on the family, successfully provide family support.

Looking back, for me, one of the greatest frustrations early on was driven by our ignorance of the mental health system, and the laws under which they must operate. For example, here in Pennsylvania, when a child turns fourteen, they are considered an adult in the mental health world. Yeah! You read that correctly.

Emily turned fourteen less than a month after her first psychiatric hospitalization. When she did, she told her mental health providers to maintain her right to privacy, and not share anything with her parents. The result? Her psychiatrist knew of many of the high-risk behaviors in which Em was involved, yet was powerless to warn us, her parents.

I was frustrated by the perceived arrogance of many in the mental health world. Rather than helping us understand the dynamics of bipolar disorder, they often gave the impression that we were the ones who were responsible for her "acting out." "I understand you have a bad temper, Mr. Brown." I may have a bad temper on occasion, but how does that help me to understand how that influences my daughter's behavior? Why not make an effort to teach me to understand?

Therein lies a major issue that our mental health services needs to address. It has been statistically proven that recovery from a mental health crisis can be greatly enhanced when the family is involved in a positive manner. Yet, as parents, we were never told that. I didn't come to understand that until I went to my first NAMI support group meeting.

Why in the world wouldn't Em's health care provider tell us? As one psychiatrist pointed out, there is no code, which psychiatrists can use to be reimbursed for family psycho education. NO CODE! How sad. A path to increased certainty of recovery is not taken because there is no code.

It felt to me as if the mental health people didn't want recovery. If someone recovers they are less dependent on mental health providers. I don't know if that is true, but I certainly perceived it that way…and perceptions can become reality.

Time and again we felt like our concern for our daughter's wellbeing was perceived as a nuisance…something they had to put up with. But there is hope and that part of the story is yet to come.

Why did it take me such a long time to respond? Pride! Denial! Maybe I simply didn't like the answer, and continued looking for one of my own. My guess is that I'm not all that unusual. Perhaps you are facing some type of crisis, and have sought some sort of help, but still feel that you probably can handle it on your own.

I have a friend whose eleven-year old son was diagnosed with a rare neurological disease. The father, who always appeared strong in his faith, became bitter towards God, especially when his son almost died

DUCT TAPE & WD-40

of cardiac arrest during his initial hospitalization. The man was looking for a miracle and couldn't see it. The miracle was his wife and her willingness to set her career aside so that she could care for their son. The miracle was in his son, who hating his suffering, did what the doctors and his mother asked of him, no matter how difficult or painful it was. The miracle was in a group of men who met each Sunday to pray for the family and especially for the father. The miracle was seen by all several months later when the son successfully played the lead part in our church's youth musical.

God always hears our prayers. In time our prayers are always answered. Our job is to "listen", then respond, whether we like the answer or not.

Chapter 9

WHEN IT DOESN'T MOVE – USE WD-40

A friend of mine said to me, "I bet you are trying to be a father to Emily like 'Father Knows Best.'" "Father Knows Best" is a very old television program. It is what I grew up with. It was representative of my father and how he raised me.

"Of course I am!"

"Yup! Bet it doesn't work, does it?"

Ouch! My friend had just hit a **raw nerve**.

My friend and I grew up together. We've known each other since fifth grade. We still live in the same town and now we have children who attend the same high school from which we graduated. My friend's son is a classmate of Emily's. That's how he knew to ask the probing question.

My friend is a recovering alcoholic. He seems to be managing his illness better these past couple of years. Nevertheless, whenever he falls off the wagon, then dries out and climbs back on, I'm one of the folks he calls. I never judge him. His illness is not something easily dealt with.

I thought that we kept in touch with one another because my role was to rescue him. Now, here he was rescuing me.

When he called to have lunch earlier that week, I simply assumed that he was back on the wagon after another fall. This was not the case. He called because he knew he could help me.

"I heard about Emily's diagnosis. I understand she is bipolar, is that right? You know that I'm bipolar, too, don't you?" I seemed to recall his having mentioned that some time in the past, although I must confess that back then I wasn't clear what that meant.

"Let me tell you what it is like growing up as a bipolar teenager in a family that was just like "Father Knows Best." And so began my understanding of what life must be like for my Emily.

I heard a lot that day, all of which opened my eyes. What helped the most was what he told me in terms of how to respond to Emily when she was acting out.

"I know you must get angry with Em when she does things that simply make no sense to you. Things that are high risk, especially."

"The first thing is to not show your anger."

Well, that was certainly helpful! He obviously didn't know how difficult that was for me. Let me rephrase that: how impossible that was for me.

"I also bet she's a good teacher, isn't she?"

"What do you mean by good teacher?" I asked.

"Em has the ability to explain complex things in simple terms, doesn't she?"

How did he know that? Adults are always amazed at her ability to interact with them in a variety of settings. For example, Em helped set up the software on the computers for one of her mom's conferences. During the conference she taught the participants (all adult teachers) how to use the software. I had many people tell me how helpful she was. It was hard to believe that she was only 14 when this happened.

"The next time you feel angry, go for a walk…do whatever is needed. Do not show your anger to Emily. Wait until you calm down. Then when you are both in a calm state of mind, ask Em to teach you! Say, 'Em, I do not understand why you do what you do. Can you help me understand? Would you teach me what it's like to be bipolar?'"

My father daughter relationship with Emily had disappeared. I didn't know how we were ever going to get it back? Now, my friend had given me the tool I needed. The tool was WD-40: If something should move and it doesn't, use WD-40 with abundance.

So what is WD-40? Listen; Learn; Help; Lead. I learned this model from Em's Uncle Newt. Newt says that when you listen to learn, you will find that people open up and share things with you. Once you learn what it is that some one really wants, you are then in a position to help them get what they want. Do this often enough and people perceive you as some one they can trust. Once they trust you, they will let you lead.

To get started, identify the primary individuals with whom you need to reconnect? Identify the opportunities for that day when you might be able to listen to learn and understand the needs of those individuals. How about your family? What is it that you feel is important to them? Now, move to thoughts of extended family, friends, and others. Is there anyone you know who is experiencing some form of hardship? You will always come in contact with people who are in great pain, but by listening you will be able to ease their suffering—and yours.

Write down any thoughts that come to mind. Make a list of things you could do to show your love.

First Rule of WD-40: to keep from damaging a relationship, or a relationship you could damage further by being angry, take a hike. That's right, just get away and let the simmer cool down. This will give you time to reflect on how to respond and it will also provide some time and space from the behavior that caused the problem.

Second Rule of WD-40: When you've calmed down, try listening. Ask an open-ended question. Then shut up and listen. "I don't understand. Can you help me to understand?"

I knew exactly what Bob was saying. The sad truth is I should have already known this. After all, I teach "trust and communications." My corporate mission is "to help organizations develop and maintain an environment of trust, where all are focused on a shared vision of hope, and each is enabled to do what it is they do best for the greater good of all." As a management consultant, I do a fair amount of training. You would think that I would practice what I preach, wouldn't you? Not when you are in denial.

There is a model for effective interpersonal relationships that I've used for years: The Johari Window. It helps people understand some of the communication problems they face as a result of conflict. It can also help them understand how to improve their interpersonal relationships.

Developed by Joe Luft and Harry Ingham, the Johari Window is a model which describes human interactions based on the idea that relationships are made up of things known and things unknown. The interaction of what is known or unknown to us, with what is known or unknown to others, leads to four descriptive areas that vitally affect all relationships.

These four areas are (see the diagram below):

- The Public Self

- Blind Self

- The Private (or hidden) Self

- The Undiscovered Self

	WHAT YOU SEE IN ME	WHAT YOU DO NOT SEE IN ME
WHAT I SEE IN ME	The Public Self	The Private (or hidden) Self
WHAT I DO NOT SEE IN ME	The Blind Self	The Undiscovered Self

The **Public Self** consists of information mutually known and shared by both people in the relationship. It includes those things which others see in us, and which we see in ourselves. We understand that the quality of relationships is directly related to the amount of information shared by both persons. The larger the arena becomes the more effective the relationship will be.

The **Blind Self** contains those things that others know about us, but about which we are unaware. A slip of the tongue or a facial response may reveal to others our thoughts, motives, etc., while we remain unaware of having communicated that information.

The **Private Self** includes those things we know about ourselves, but which we choose to keep private from everyone else. As two people open up to each other it is the blind self and the private self that provide immediate opportunity for enlarging the public self.

Finally, the **Undiscovered Self** is that aspect of a person about which neither person knows. As this is reduced through open communication it represents the greatest "potential" for self-discovery.

The fact is: *you are the one responsible for the quality and effectiveness of your interpersonal relationships and for the benefits that can be gained for maintaining open communication.*

It is obvious that people communicate more effectively in an enlarged public self. The reasons are:

- You work a lot less at keeping up a private self.

- There are fewer problems dealing with new, novel, or threatening information.

- People reduce the tension between them, thereby being better able to understand one another.

- The larger the Public Self, the better the opportunity for creating a higher level of trust. This will open up the possibility of a better relationship.

As soon as I asked Emily to help me understand, I began to drop my defenses. As I learned more about Em, my public self expanded greatly, and so did hers.

Things didn't change quickly. As matter of fact, I can still recall Emily's response when I said to her, "Em, I don't understand. Would you teach me what it is like to be bipolar?" "Sure, Dad! Whatever!" It was as if she was saying to herself, "Here we go again! Don't worry! He just came up with a new idea. He'll soon get over it!"

Chapter 11 tells more about what happened next. The important thing to note here is that recovery is possible. Not only is recovery possible, you can have a direct impact upon that recovery.

Despite Em's immediate response, from that day on we started our journey back to a relationship built on trust. She soon became delighted with my new approach. It took awhile, but gradually she came to trust that I would not get angry...at least not explosively angry. She enjoyed teaching me because I was a good student. She helped me under-stand why she would sometimes hurt herself by cutting or burning herself. "Physical pain, Dad, is the Advil for emotional turbulence." She explained her hyper-sensitive hearing to me. She helped me see just how fast her brain would process information from time to time. I eventually came to accept her world, knowing that I would never totally understand it. The biggest victory seems to be that I stopped judging her world, and more importantly, I stopped judging Emily.

Third Rule of WD-40: Listen to learn. Learn to help. There was a needlepoint that hung in Uncle Newt's office: "Listen, Learn, Help, Lead." As I mentioned before, it is one of the models of leadership that Newt used so successfully in his political career. If you listen to learn, you'll begin to better understand the true needs of the individual who is talking. When you begin to understand the true needs of another, you are then in a position to help them meet those needs. As you help people meet their own needs, they, in turn, become more willing to let you lead for you have proven yourself worthy of their trust.

You help when you make yourself available to another and that is usually the help they are seeking.

Before my friend and I had our conversation, I was a father using one-way communication. I simply stated what I expected then attempted to hold Emily accountable to my expectations, especially in her academic performance. I had failed to practice that which I taught others about good communication, and about good relationships.

When I switched from one-way to two-way communication, our world, our family living together became brighter, friendlier, and more hopeful.

We must not forget about your WD-40. Your writing will tell you which relationships are stuck and which ones need the most help. Having identified those relationships, what comes next?

Like duct tape, WD-40 also comes in all shapes and sizes, but here are some suggestions:

- Write your loved one a letter. This will allow you to say what you want to say without getting tongue-tied.

- Make a date. Maybe a quiet dinner is a place to start or just take a walk together.

- How about a twenty-four-hour getaway? Go to a place that will allow you to be quiet and reflective.

- You might try an escape weekend somewhere you know your loved one would enjoy.

- Take off early from work and spend time with your loved one.

- Whatever shape or form your WD-40 takes on, be sure and include the key ingredient: enough time and your undivided attention.

When the stage is set and the time is right, simply say, "Please, forgive me. I know I've been a real jerk. I'm sorry if I have hurt you in any way." Then, while they sit there in a state of shock, go on to say, "I have missed you. How have you been?" Then shut up and listen.

WD-40! When you discover and use yours, it will work wonders!

Chapter 10

THINGS I DIDN'T KNOW BEFORE!

A person dies by suicide every eighteen minutes in the United States. With every suicide, there are family members, friends, and co-workers left behind to cope with this tragic loss and try to make sense out of it. Sixty to ninety percent of all people who commit suicide have a diagnosable psychiatric or psychological disorder at the time of their death.

Every year in the U.S. more people die of suicide in this nation then of HIV AIDS.

Where then is the government funded research, the fundraisers, and the celebrity spokesperson for suicide?

From the Interim Report of President Bush's New Freedom Commission on Mental Health:

The disability toll can be quantified in a way that cannot be ignored: when compared with all other diseases (such as cancer and heart disease), mental illness ranks first in terms of causing disability in the United States, Canada, and Western Europe, according to a study by the World Health Organization (WHO, 2001). This groundbreaking study found that mental illness (including depression, bipolar disorder, and schizophrenia) accounts for 25% of all disability across major industrialized countries.

Mental illness is shockingly common, affecting almost every American family — directly or indirectly. It can strike a child, a brother, a grandparent, or a co-worker. It can strike someone of any background — white, African American, Asian American, Pacific Islander, Hispanic American, or Native American. It can strike at any stage of life, from childhood to old age. No community is unaffected, no school or workplace untouched.

Studies show women are most affected by depression. About 5-7% of adults, in a given year, have a serious mental illness, according to several nationally representative studies.

I never knew any of these statistics four years ago. I began thinking back upon my mother-in-law's mental illness with a whole new perspective. But suicide? That would never happen in my family ... would it?

Then came May 18, 2000. There, but for the grace of God go I. My Emily had attempted suicide.

Dramatic improvements in care and treatments have developed in the last ten years. Mental health diagnosis and treatments have benefited from new medications, modern science, and clinical advancements.

Mental illnesses include such disorders as schizophrenia, schizoaffective disorder, bipolar disorder, major depressive disorder, obsessive-compulsive disorder, panic and other severe anxiety disorders, pervasive developmental disorders, attention deficit/hyperactivity disorder, borderline personality disorder, and other severe and persistent mental illnesses that affect the brain.

These disorders can profoundly disrupt a person's thinking, feeling, moods, ability to relate to others, and capacity for coping with the demands of life.

Mental illnesses are treatable. Most people with serious mental illness need medication to help control symptoms, but also rely on supportive counseling, self-help groups, assistance with housing, vocational rehabilitation, income assistance, and other community services in order to achieve their highest level of recovery.

NAMI provided me with some important facts about mental illness and recovery:

- Mental illnesses are biologically-based brain disorders. They cannot be overcome through "will power" and are not related to a person's "character" or intelligence.

- Mental illnesses strike individuals in the prime of their lives, often during adolescence and young adulthood. All ages are susceptible, but the young and the old are especially vulnerable.

- Without treatment the consequences of mental illness for the individual and society are staggering: unnecessary disability, unemployment, substance abuse, homelessness, inappropriate incarceration, suicide, and wasted lives.

- The best treatments for serious mental illnesses today are highly effective; between seventy and ninety percent of individuals have significant reduction of symptoms and improved quality of life with a combination of pharmacological and psychosocial treatments and supports.

97

- Early identification and treatment is of vital importance; by getting people the treatment they need early, recovery is accelerated and the brain is protected from further harm related to the course of illness.

- Stigma erodes confidence that mental disorders are real, treatable health conditions. We have allowed stigma and a now unwarranted sense of hopelessness to erect attitudinal, structural, and financial barriers to effective treatment and recovery. It is time to take these barriers down.

What is bipolar disorder?

Bipolar disorder, or manic depression, is a serious brain disorder that causes extreme shifts in mood, energy, and functioning. It affects 2.3 million adult Americans, which is about 1.2 percent of the population, and can run in families. The disorder affects men and women equally. Bipolar disorder is characterized by episodes of mania and depression that can last from days to months. Bipolar disorder is a chronic and generally lifelong condition with recurring episodes that often begin in adolescence or early adulthood, and occasionally, even in children. It generally requires lifelong treatment, and recovery between episodes is often poor. Generally, those who suffer from bipolar disorder have symptoms of both mania and depression (sometimes at the same time).

What are the symptoms of mania?

Mania is the word that describes the activated phase of bipolar disorder. The symptoms of mania may include:

- either an elated, happy mood or an irritable, angry, unpleasant mood

- increased activity or energy

- more thoughts and faster thinking than normal

- increased talking, more rapid speech than normal

- ambitious, often grandiose, plans

- poor judgment

- increased sexual interest and activity

- decreased sleep and decreased need for sleep

What are the symptoms of depression?

Depression is the other phase of bipolar disorder. The symptoms of depression may include:

- depressed or apathetic mood

- decreased activity and energy

- restlessness and irritability

- fewer thoughts than usual and slowed thinking

- less talking and slowed speech

- less interest or participation in, and less enjoyment of activities

- decreased sexual interest and activity

- hopeless and helpless feelings

- feelings of guilt and worthlessness

- pessimistic outlook

- thoughts of suicide

- change in appetite (either eating more or eating less)

- change in sleep patterns (either sleeping more or sleeping less)

What is a "mixed" state?

A mixed state is when symptoms of mania and depression occur at the same time. During a mixed state, depressed mood accompanies manic activation.

What are the causes of bipolar disorder?

While the exact cause of bipolar disorder is not known, most researchers believe it is the result of a chemical imbalance in certain parts of the brain. Other evidence suggests that the disorder results from impairments of the function of intracellular signaling pathways (the "machinery" inside nerve cells) within specific areas of the brain. Scientists have found evidence of a genetic predisposition to the illness. Bipolar disorder tends to run in families, and close relatives of someone with bipolar disorder are more likely to be affected. It is important to note that bipolar episodes can and often do occur without any obvious trigger.

How is bipolar disorder treated?

While there is no cure for bipolar disorder, it is a treatable and manageable illness. After an accurate diagnosis, most people can be successfully treated. Medication is an essential part of successful treatment. Maintenance treatment with a mood stabilizer substantially reduces the number and severity of episodes for most people, although episodes of mania or depression may occur and require a specific additional treatment. In addition, psychosocial therapies including, cognitive-behavioral therapy, interpersonal therapy, family therapy, and psycho-education are important to help people understand the illness and to develop skills to cope with the stresses that can trigger episodes.

Medications used to treat mania. Medications commonly used to treat manic episodes of bipolar disorder are called *mood stabilizers.*

Medications used to treat depression. During depressive episodes, people with bipolar disorder may need additional treatment with an antidepressant medication. Because of the risk of triggering mania, doctors often prescribe an antidepressant only after the individual is already receiving a therapeutic dose of lithium or an anticonvulsant mood stabilizer.

Patients and their families must be cautious during the early stages of treatment when energy levels and the ability to take action return before mood improves. At this time – when decisions are easier to make, but depression is still severe – the risk of suicide may temporarily increase.

What are the side effects of the medications used to treat bipolar disorder?

All medications have side effects. Different medications produce different side effects, and people differ in the amount and severity of side effects they experience.

Side effects of medications used to treat mania. Side effects of lithium include hand tremors, excessive thirst, excessive urination, and memory problems. Side effects often become less troublesome after a few weeks as the body adjusts to the medication.

Common side effects of anticonvulsant mood stabilizers include nausea, drowsiness, dizziness, and tremors.

Side effects of medications used to treat depression. About half of the people taking antidepressant medications have mild side effects during the first few weeks of treatment.

Now, remember you feel the way you feel because, as hard as you try, you cannot control another person's behavior. The more you try, the worse it gets. So why not stop trying. This is what it is like to throw in the towel, except, in this case, you don't lose the fight, you *both* win.

Don't let all this new information scare you. If you have a loved one who suffers from a mental illness remember, mental illnesses, like other illnesses, are treatable. There is hope for recovery. You can make a difference in the recovery process of your loved one.

Chapter 11

EMILY REVISITED

It had been months since I started changing the way I communicated with Emily. I would start every day the same way with duct tape and WD-40. I focused on my perceived mission. "My mission is to create a safe home, emotionally; a home to which we can all return to at the end of the day in a sense of peace and joy." I would put my pen down and focus. When I focus on something written it helps me to block out other competing thoughts.

I was looking for a WD-40 miracle. As hard as I tried, it seemed as if I was making no headway at all. Emily still exhibited behaviors that would trigger my anger: She stayed home from school with increased frequency; she pushed the envelope with her public displays of affection for her boyfriend; and, she came to take pleasure in saying some of the most bizarre things simply to shock people.

There were things she did that frightened me to no end. She called me from her mobile phone in the middle of a school day to tell me that she didn't know where she was. She said that she was in the woods somewhere, and that it felt as if she bumped her head on something.

How did I respond? I did something that was both brilliant and stupid. My mind raced trying to think of the possible places she may have been. If she had left school in the morning, then I had a good idea of where she was. However, if she had gone to her vo-tech school like she was scheduled to, where she was studying Microsoft systems, I'd be less certain of where she was. What was brilliant was the question I asked: "Emily, what sounds do you hear?" She replied that she could hear cars "not too far away." That was brilliant because it helped me confirm my original suspicions. She was probably at a wooded area a few blocks from our home that is called, "the jumps." It has been a favorite hang out for kids over the years. They have created some very intricate bike paths and jumps. It is a place that she would go to on her own. It is a place less than a mile from where I was.

What was stupid? For some reason, I told her to hang up and walk toward the sounds, then call me when she got there. Now, that was stupid. My administrative assistant, who by now was very much aware of the potential for all types of strange calls from Emily, looked at me and asked, "Why did you tell her to hang up? What if she doesn't call back?" I simply stared at her in total shock over my own stupidity and silently prayed that God keep Emily safe.

It seemed like forever until the phone rang again, but it was Emily and she was excited. "I know where I am Dad. I'm at the jumps."

"Walk out to the street and wait, Em. I'm on my way."

I should have kept her on the line while I was driving, just to keep her assured that she would be okay. But stupid me, I hung up. Instead, I called her psychiatrist's office while I headed to pick her up. Their advice was to bring her there for a quick evaluation.

In a couple of minutes I saw Em standing along side the road. She got in the car and we hugged. I told her that her doctor wanted to see her right away. She shrugged her shoulders as we drove away.

"Help me understand, Em, how did you end up at the jumps? When did you leave school?" The last thing she said that she remembered was walking home at lunchtime rather than getting on the bus for vo-tech. "I just couldn't stand the thought of being trapped in that school this afternoon, so I went home. But how I got to the jumps, I don't know. I simply don't have any memory of that."

In less than five minutes after her psychiatrist called her in, he came out with a prescription for an immediate drug evaluation. "She is exhibiting behaviors that are often associated with some type of illegal drug. We need to know if that's the case before we decide what needs to be done."

"Drugs?" I felt that one in the pit of my stomach. "Please, God. Don't let her test positive for drugs!"

She said, "Dad, don't worry. I don't do drugs." Well, time will tell, won't it?

She was right. She tested negatively for drugs. She simply experienced a blackout of sorts, where she had no memory of what she was doing. Is this another new twist in what I have to watch for and worry about?

The next morning my prayers were more prayers of panic than anything. "God, why are you not answering my prayers? Every day, day after day, I ask for healing for Emily's emotions. Lost in the woods? Do you call that healing?"

A couple of weeks later I get the call from high school. "Mr. Brown, the principal wants to see you."

"When?" I asked.

"Immediately!" the principal's secretary replied.

"Can you give me some hint as to why?" I asked.

"Alcohol on school property," they replied.

Alcohol? My Emily? At school?

Talk about flashbacks. As a senior at the very same high school many years before, I, too, was confronted by the principal over the issue of alcohol. It was on our senior trip to New York City and the World's Fair in 1964. When we arrived at the fair, a group of us had already planned to jump a subway to downtown, NYC.

We hit New York with a vengeance, stopping at the very first bar we came to. No one asked for ID. They simply gave us what we asked for…beer and lots of it.

By the time we got back to the fair we were all rather inebriated. I remember falling on the steps getting back into the bus that was taking us to our hotel. A couple of my more sober friends quickly got me up on my feet and back to a seat before I made a greater fool of myself. A couple hours later we were in our hotel rooms, and I was dropping water balloons on people below, having a great time of it, too. Then, much to my chagrin, I noticed the principal standing on the other side of the street, taking note of who was dropping water balloons. I was the one he saw.

Within moments he was pounding on our door. "Brown, I suggest you get in bed immediately and stay there. If you choose not to, and you continue doing the stupid things you are doing, I will put you on a bus headed home with a phone call to your parents. Do I make myself understood?"

I guess I shouldn't be shocked at my daughter's flirtation with alcohol. That's all it was, I hoped.

When I got to the principal's office, Emily was curled up in the fetal position, expecting the very worst from me. But thankfully, she didn't get what she expected. I sat and listened to the principal explain that Emily had brought a coke bottle, flavored with a fair amount of Windsor Canadian Whiskey, onto the vo-tech school bus and was passing it around to her friends.

Emily's explanation? There was none. She simply said she was sorry.

An automatic two-week suspension! Little did the school realize that this was not a punishment for Emily. This was a vacation from the place she hated most.

I was right. It was a one-time episode. Emily decided on her own that drugs and alcohol would only make her mysterious behaviors all the more unpredictable.

Lost in the woods? Taking alcohol on the school bus? There were others but you get the point. This prayer thing didn't seem to be working. Emily wasn't getting better. If anything, she seemed to be getting worse.

Yet every day, day after day, I would pray a focused and reflective prayer, asking for healing, asking for help.

Fall turned into winter, winter into spring. It had now been two years since Emily's suicide attempt. I had been praying my focused reflective prayers for almost a year.

Emily calls me again, from her vo-tech School. "Dad, I'm in the girl's room. I have taken the shoelaces off my boots, wrapped them around my neck, and tied them to the top of the stall. I'm standing on the commode. All I want to do is to jump."

I sat there in total composure, as if I had expected this type of call. I asked Emily to help me understand, while I wrote a note to my assistant. "Call the school and tell them that Emily is in the girl's room and needs their help." As she placed the call I asked Emily if she wanted me to come get her. "Yes, Dad, yes. Get me out of this hell hole."

I kept her on the phone till I could hear help arrive. It was then that I hung up and started to shake with fear. I drove to the school, walked right past the security guy who was up out of his seat in panic. I went right to the office and talked with the principal. He took me to where they were keeping Em. I took her hand and said let's go. I didn't ask anyone for permission to take my daughter out of the school. I simply marched her out, right past the security post. While he was still insisting that I should sign in, I took her out to the car.

We sat in the car for half an hour. "Emily, help me understand…"

She sat there in tears telling me how horrid that place was. She told me how uncaring people were. She told me how incompetent her teachers were. She cried and cried. I simply sat there with my hand on her shoulder waiting for her to stop. I didn't say anything. I didn't tell her that she was wrong, or that she simply didn't see things the way she ought to see them. I didn't tell her anything other than to reassure her of my love.

After she settled down, I asked her what she thought we should do. I knew she should be hospitalized. I was surprised the school hadn't called for her hospitalization.

Emily's first response! "I suppose we could go home and just pretend this didn't happen."

"That's one option," I replied. "Any others?"

"Dad, I hate the thought of going back to a hospital."

"I understand, Em. That first time was not a real positive experience. How about if we find out if there are other hospitals available, so that you wouldn't have to see that place again?"

"Okay" Em said with tears running down her face. "Let's go. I really need help!" as she began to sob.

It wasn't until two or three days later that I could see God's hand in all of this. We had Emily placed in a hospital that was ninety miles away, in a country setting. It was a very peaceful place, at least from the outside. They had several buildings on campus, one for each age group, and each degree of severity in behaviors. Emily came out of her building with a smile on her face proclaiming, "Dad, the kids here are really sick!"

"No kidding, Em? This is a psychiatric hospital. What did you expect?"

"Dad, don't get me wrong. I'm sick, too. It's just that I know that I'm sick. They don't. They're still blaming their parents."

It was all I could do to keep from crying. Emily had a major breakthrough. She acknowledged her illness for the first time. She turned a corner. By the grace of God, she was headed toward recovery.

It took another year till my hopes became reality. We enrolled her into a special school her junior year. It was a school that specialized in the education of students suffering from some form of mental illness. This, too, was an answer to prayer.

When we started looking for a school, we had no idea how we would pay for such a place. Our web search told us to expect tuitions of over $40,000 per year. When I turned to God the next morning, He told me to call a friend; a very special friend that he introduced me to many years ago. He reminded me of this friend who was now the Executive Director of our Intermediate Unit, the entity that helps school districts deal with special needs.

My friend was more than willing to help. He told me that they had a program just for kids like Emily. They operate their program using space in one of the area school districts, giving the kids a sense of attending a real school. They provide psychiatric and psychological services in addition to teaching. Emily wouldn't have to go away. They would come pick her up every day and bring her home after school was out. And best of all! It was free. Our tax dollars paid for this service.

As I write this part of our story, we are ten days away from high school graduation. Emily has taken responsibility for the management of her illness. She manages her prescriptions. She listens to the advice of those who counsel her. She has learned how to cope.

Nine months ago she mainstreamed back into the same school that she started in twelve years ago. In ten days, she will graduate with her class.

It has been a journey that I will never forget. Emily? She wants to tell you about the ending herself. She simply prefers to do so in the "blogasphere". Log on to www.ducttapeandwe40.com and ask her yourself.

As for me, my faith in God has grown beyond my own understanding. I stated in the first chapter that God told me to write this book. Perhaps now you understand what I meant.

A young man from a neighboring school district killed himself last month. He was a star athlete, honor roll student, with lots of friends. He was accepted into college this fall, yet for some unknown reason he decided to kill himself.

Depression is a very real illness. But there is hope. There is recovery. People need to know that. God uses people like me to help others know that there is hope and there is recovery. That's why He used my gifts so that someone who has read this far will put down this book and pick up the phone or goes to the web willing at least to look for help.

If you are that person, my prayers are with you. Please let us know so that we can add you to our prayer list. The more people who pray, asking for help, the greater the sense of hope you will have as you make your way back to recovery.

Some one once said, "Everything is okay in the end. If it's not okay, then it is not the end."

6-7-04: From my personal prayer journal ... my "Duct Tape" ...

My prayer today is one of immense thanksgiving. I'm thankful for Emily's strength of character that has carried her from the depths of so many high-risk behaviors driven by her bipolar disorder to the heights of graduation today.

Emily's journey has had a profound impact upon my own life, forcing me to acknowledge cruel realities. It felt, at times, as if I were watching a horrible movie about another little girl; for the little girl that I knew as a father had died, but was not buried. Who was this person who spoke so openly about her own sexuality, shocking all who would hear? Who was this person who attempted to kill herself; who spent hours upon hours surfing the web seeking some of the most morbid images; who was this person who enticed a young man to come and visit for two weeks, all the way from Scotland; who called me one day telling me she was lost in the woods; who called me one evening from a motel asking for a ride home, realizing she shouldn't be there; who sat in the principals office facing a two week suspension for taking alcohol on the school bus; who called me from school threatening suicide once again... Who was she?

Today is a milestone, marking a huge victory on her journey out of that horrid past. Thanks be to God she was moved to accept the fact that she suffers from a mental illness. She learned ways of coping with her illness. She took responsibility for her own meds. She learned to tolerate the very school district that had rejected her and spit her out three years before. She developed the courage needed to march back into that school, smile at those who scorned her, who mocked her, and to do all that the school asked her to do simply so she could march with her class today.

I am so very proud of her progress, of her courage, of her willingness to never give up.

I do not know what lies in her future. But I do know that based upon this past year, whatever Emily sets her heart upon, she will do it. She will succeed.

She has a marvelous gift for words. God will use her in some way, some day, to impact the world. It won't always be fun. There is always the risk that the disorder will take over once again. But her disorder is part of her gifts for it will be the manic energy that will move her to new heights whatever they may be.

Whatever path she chooses, I will cheer her, for she is my Emily and I love her. As her father, I will always love her.

Written in the Spirit of prayer. Thank You, Father, for my Emily.

Love,

David

Philippians 4: 6-7

Chapter 12

NOW WHAT? NOW IT'S YOUR TURN!

Is it possible to make sense out of the illogical? Somehow, I want to try. Why? Because there is another dad out there just like me; or should I say, just like the dad I used to be. He's struggling with the knowledge that a child of his hated life so much that all he or she wanted to do was to end it. He's angry at the system. He's devastated by dreams lost. He feels guilty, but doesn't know why. He can't focus at work. Unknowingly, he slips into a deep depression himself. His work suffers; his family suffers; his friends don't have a clue. I remember my accountant telling me, "It's been a year, David. It's time to snap out of it and get on with life."

God told me to write this book. I never questioned God as to why. I simply started to write. Page after page the story would flow, without regard to why. I simply wrote.

How can I be so certain that God told me to write this book?

It started in November 2001. Five months into my regimen of focused, reflective prayers, a friend of mine met me for lunch. He was intrigued by my frequent reference to my prayer journal in Sunday school class. He is a journalist himself. I didn't know about his struggles in life at the time. I simply elaborated upon my use of a prayer journal in response to his questions.

"You should write a book," he said. "There are people out there that need to hear your story."

I was intrigued with the thought. I must confess I have often thought about writing a book. I just never knew what it was I should write.

The morning after this lunch experience, I wrote in my journal, "Lord, if I am to write, lead me to write." I focused. I reflected. Nothing.

I would repeat this prayer from time to time over the next several months, always to the same end. Nothing. For two years I would pray this prayer. Nothing.

Then one day, in November of 2003, the title, "Duct Tape and WD 40," came out of nowhere. I remember writing it in my journal, then wondering what in the world it meant. Day after day, I would focus and reflect in prayer, asking for wisdom and understanding. Slowly but surely, the concept of this book began to take place.

Then God spoke loud and clear. Well, he didn't actually speak. He left a not too subtle clue.

It was the weekend before Thanksgiving. My daughter, Susan, needed a ride up north to church camp for a winter retreat. Camp Krislund is two hours north of our home, close to State College, Pennsylvania, the home of Penn State University. My wife and I thought it would be a good excuse to spend a couple of nights on our own, so we agreed to drive Susan and her friend up to camp.

Before we left town, Susan asked if we would stop at Rite Aid. If there is one thing this father has learned is never ask why his daughter wants to stop at a drug store. He simply forks over ten dollars and let's her get what she sees as necessary. In this case, it was a roll of duct tape.

The whole way north, I could hear Susan and her friend laughing and giggling in the back seat. On occasion, I'd hear the sounds of a piece of duct tape being ripped from the roll. Lo and behold, by the time we arrived at camp, the two of them had made duct tape wallets, the latest of fads at the time.

It was a moonless night, and when you are in the woods it is dark. We unloaded the girls' things in the dark, finding our way to the recreation center where they checked in. Making sure that all was well, it was hugs and kisses, then on our way to our own weekend retreat in State College.

While unloading the car in the parking lot of our hotel, I almost lost my breath. My prayer journal and Bible were in the back in the same area as their camping things. Sticking to my prayer journal was the label from the duct tape roll. Some call it a coincidence. I don't believe in coincidence. My faith tells me that things happen for a reason. This was God's not so subtle clue.

"Write the book, David!" I knew better than to ask why.

It took me a month to get started. I would pray for clarity. I would pray for understanding. I would pray for wisdom. I would pray for courage. Writing was a scary proposition for me. I had never written anything other than short articles.

Then on December 22, 2003, at two o'clock in the morning, I woke up with the first chapter racing in my mind. I got up, got dressed, made a pot of coffee, read scripture, prayed, and went to my office. The first chapter flowed from me like hot lava down the side of a volcano. I didn't do an outline. I didn't mind map my thoughts. I simply typed.

God gave me a daughter who saw the value in telling the story, giving me her permission to tell it all. Friends rallied around me without my asking. Each encouraged me in their own way. Now do you understand why I believe God told me to write this book?

Let me repeat what I said earlier: This book is for the father like me, for mothers and siblings, for the family like mine. This book is for the teen like Emily, who doesn't know how to tell his or her father or mother what they really feel; that they are so afraid of life, they don't know how they can go on living. This book is for the friend of that father, the friend who can see what is happening, but has no way of telling the dad. This book is for the grandparent watching their son live a life of hell and doesn't have a clue what to do.

I am overwhelmed every time I speak to an audience about this story. One of the questions I have come to ask is, "How many people, here, tonight, know of someone who suffers from a mental illness?" Every time, at least seventy-five to ninety percent of the people raise their hands.

If most of us know of someone who suffers, then why in the world don't we talk about it? Stigma!

Someone sent me information about NAMI a couple of months after Emily's diagnosis. I opened the envelope, saw the words mental illness, and immediately put it away. That unwillingness on my part to accept the truth cost me a year of my life. It cost me thousands of dollars in lost income. That's my story.

Now, multiply my story by millions more. The impact that stigma has upon this nation of ours is enormous. Not only does it impact the quality of life of those who suffer, but also the lives of all those they touch.

What if business was to measure this impact against their bottom lines? How is their productivity affected? How many lost days of work? What is the error rate of distracted workers?

It doesn't have to be this way. My Emily is proof positive. She started college recently with the goal of attaining the dean's list. Her early grades prove that she is serious. I watch her study in a way I never saw before. She enjoys learning. She enjoys her life. She is able to do this because she accepted her illness for what it is, an illness – one that can be treated.

Recovery is possible. It's hard work. It requires on going pharmaceutical treatment under the watchful eye of a skilled psychiatrist. It requires the willingness of a loved one to work with the one who suffers, attempting to insure there is an environment conducive to recovery. It takes patience on everyone's part. It takes time.

Recovery is possible, but you have to take that first step. For me, it was prayer. God gave me a friend who made me aware of what it is like to be a teenager who suffers from manic depression, this friend who told me what he wishes his father would have done differently. God led me to NAMI's course, Family-to-Family, which taught me how to do what my friend told me to do.

That's my story. But it doesn't end there. It doesn't end with just me. Now it is your turn. There are many things in this book for you to reflect upon and try. Discover what works for you and then stick to it like duct tape.

You are a part of this story because God told me to write this book so that you, too, could be helped. Where are the struggles you face in your relationships? WD-40 will work wonders.

My prayer for you is that duct tape and WD-40 will be two valuable tools that will make it happen for you. The end result will hopefully be a new and healthier life for each of you and those you love.

I know that although I awoke this morning and that life was beautiful once again, I never know what lies around the bend.

With duct tape and WD-40 I'm ready for whatever the river of life puts in my way, white water rapids and all.

That's it. Pretty simple, isn't it? Duct Tape – coming to better understand myself and my relationships and WD-40 – being there for others. Two different things but they go hand in hand.

I never expected miracles and there were times that I felt as if it wasn't worth the effort. "Sure Dad! Whatever!" But I learned to trust what was happening. Changing behavior takes time. One bad day now and then is no reason to stop trying.

Duct tape and WD-40! Use it every day. The people in your life will thank you - and love you.

THINGS I CONTINUE TO LEARN

As the father of a daughter who suffers from bipolar disorder, a mental illness, formerly know as manic depression, I reflect on what has brought me to this point in my life. It is now four years after my daughter's suicide attempt and subsequent hospitalization. My daughter has learned how to manage her illness and has recently achieved some of her goals that we thought were impossible just two years ago.

I thank God every day for sparing Emily's life, for telling her to pick up the phone and call 911.

My daughter's journey convinces me that there is hope for recovery when mental illness rudely interrupts a family's journey through life. I am also convinced that many suicides can be prevented.

This poem was written the day after Em and I had made our first public appearance as a father and daughter team. We spoke at the NAMI PA's annual conference in Pittsburgh in the fall of 2004, telling our story to a group of parents and health care providers. One of the workshop participants asked Emily, "with today's advances in gene therapy, if there was a chance to modify or eliminate the root cause of your illness, would you take it?" Emily quickly replied "No"; because, if she did, she wouldn't be Emily. Now that's a statement of high self esteem. That's the sign of a healthy state of mind.

Out of that cathartic experience came this poem. Emily said, "It doesn't have a title, I really couldn't think of one."

They were trying to make me a martyr, I realized. Why only now?

> At thirteen I realized life was a joke
> "Burnout" the people thought
> I was sure of this
> As mall-walkers glanced at me
> And my worn expression
> The cigarette dangling haphazardly from my lips
> Periodically dusting ash on a well worn cardigan
> Hid my age concealed my girlhood from prying eyes
> Leading them to believe I was a product of the
> So-called "Generation X"
> When faded denim and t-shirts featuring
> Obscure bands became a symbol of wisdom
> Arcane knowledge and experience I'll never know
> Standing on tables at parties wouldn't get their attention
> They were immune to the fucking and drinking and fighting
> It wasn't their responsibility it wasn't their scene
> I wasn't their ward
> I stood staring blankly expressionless with wonder
> In awe of their ability to overlook the flares I shot
> From the gun stored snugly in my hip pocket
> Nestled next to that pack of cigarettes and a stolen lighter
> I raised my flag safety orange not white with surrender
> Defiance was my name and I stood in their face

Unrelenting in the struggle to find a cure for ignorance
At seventeen it seemed hopeless
To continue to struggle when I saw that the
Cutting and screaming small scale theft and promiscuity
Weren't illustrating the point
The crowds far too occupied with slaughtering the messenger
They lost the missive
So I sit down and shut up pen in hand to find myself
Withdrawn again I know I'm slipping in and out of sleep
In a booth in a diner at four in the morning
The intendment lost for years now seems of such importance
To those who turned away from my desperate solicitation
I stood before them explaining my plight
And they sat in rapture in awe of my bravery
Shed tears of empathy trying to latch onto the misery
I'd long since forgotten
At eighteen I knew that life was a joke
"Hero" they said
And I doubted this
As consumers and patients looked towards me
How an embittered and jaded girl with
Faded denim and t-shirts featuring
Obscure bands became a martyr I'll never know.

—Emily M. Brown

"Life results from the non-random survival
of randomly varying replicators."
–Richard Dawkins

123

I was amazed by that experience. Public speaking has been part of my career for almost thirty years, so I felt somewhat relaxed before the presentation. Em is a novice when it comes to speaking. However, it's obvious to this proud parent that she has inherited the gift. She intuitively knows how to hold the audience in rapt attention.

I coached Em on who the audience was. I never told her what to say, nor did I suggest what she should say. I simply told her to keep in mind the people to whom she was talking.

After I told the story, much like I have already written in this book, I turned to Em and said, "We'll Em, that's my story. I'm sure they want to hear yours." I then stepped to the side and watched in awe as this then eighteen year old took control of the audience.

Then she hooked me. "Dad would forever and always ask me what it was like to think like me. At first, I assumed that he had just read another one of those books on mental health issues, and he was trying some manipulative technique that I know him to do from time to time. However, after a few weeks, his persistent requests began to sound sincere. It was only then that I became free to ask myself, 'Why do I do the things I do?' I never asked myself that kind of question because I was to busy defending myself from the onslaught of ignorant people who just didn't have a clue. For the first time, someone important in my life began to ask for my point of view rather than telling me theirs. That was extremely liberating."

I simply stood and stared at her with tears in my eyes. She never told me what she was telling this room full of strangers. I'll always take validation no matter what form it comes in, when or where.

The road to recovery is a never-ending road. I watch Em struggle with her mood swings, knowing that it is her struggle, not mine. All I can do is hug her and let her know I'm there if she needs me. We still go to camp from time to time. Sometimes we go to lunch together and talk about whatever is current in either of our lives. I try to be as open about my life as I can, as if we were friends, not father daughter. She still knows when I disapprove of some of her decisions or actions; however, those instances are few and far between.

It was my honor and privilege to drive Em to Boston recently so she could tour Emerson College. Emerson is for students gifted in the arts, especially the art of communication. They specialize in the performing arts, the art of the written word, the art of the spoken word, and the use of all types of media in the fields of communication. She has forever and always been fascinated by film.

Em sent me a thank you note after we got home acknowledging my supportive role in her life. She even recalled the day when she was an elementary school student that she produced her first video. She recruited a couple of friends and her sister to be the actors in Hansel and Gretel. She had a script she had written and was directing as well as acting in this production. "You were my first cameraman, Dad."

It was a seven-hour drive up and seven hours back the next day. I thought for sure that Em would sleep most of the way, as she tends to do when we make those long work trips up to Maine each summer. But, it was just the two of us this time, and she honored me with her company.

We talked about movies. We talked about music. She taught me the history of heavy metal rock. (Please don't ask me about this topic. I'll admit that I didn't have a clue about much of what she was telling me.)

We talked about the past the two of us shared. "Em, help me understand why you feigned illness so often on school days. Was it because you had some form of fear you were avoiding?" That was always my assumption.

"No dad. I was never afraid of school. I was just so depressed at times that I simply couldn't get myself out of bed."

How freeing it is to have an open and accepting relationship today. I never cease to be amazed at the things I continue to learn about what it must be like to suffer from bipolar disorder.

Once in Every Life

Once in every life
There comes someone
Who opens the inner door
And speaks to the heart and soul,
Who touches you so completely
So exquisitely
Their sweet passing
Changes your life...forever.

In that one brief moment,
That one person reminds you
Everything you have hoped for can be realized;
Everything you have dreamed of can come true
Everything you have waited for
Is now waiting for you.

The purpose of their coming
And touching you so deeply
Was not that you change them,
Or they change you,
But that you remember
The gift that is you
And the love you have to share.

Once in every life
There comes someone so special
Who gives you the gift of your freedom
And the courage to reach for who you are.

— James S. Nelson, 1995

TreeNeutral™

Advantage Media Group is proud to be a part of the Tree Neutral™ program. Tree Neutral offsets the number of trees consumed in the production and printing of this book by taking proactive steps such as planting trees in direct proportion to the number of trees used to print books. To learn more about Tree Neutral, please visit **www. treeneutral.com**. To learn more about Advantage Media Group's commitment to being a responsible steward of the environment, please visit **www.advantagefamily.com/green**

Printed in the United States
210405BV00001B/373-558/P

9 781599 320908